# FORECASTING OPPORTUNITY

*Kairos*, Production, and Writing

Hunter W. Stephenson

University Press of America,® Inc.
Lanham · Boulder · New York · Toronto · Oxford

Copyright © 2005 by
University Press of America,® Inc.
4501 Forbes Boulevard
Suite 200
Lanham, Maryland 20706
UPA Acquisitions Department (301) 459-3366

PO Box 317
Oxford
OX2 9RU, UK

All rights reserved
Printed in the United States of America
British Library Cataloging in Publication Information Available

Library of Congress Control Number: 2005921315

ISBN: 978-0-7618-3161-7

⊖™ The paper used in this publication meets the minimum
requirements of American National Standard for Information
Sciences—Permanence of Paper for Printed Library Materials,
ANSI Z39.48—1984

# Contents

|       | Preface                                     | v   |
|-------|---------------------------------------------|-----|
| One   | *Kairos*: Construct and Metaphor            | 1   |
| Two   | *Kairos*: Tool and Force                    | 15  |
| Three | *Kairos* Outside the Domain of Rhetoric     | 33  |
| Four  | Timing and Proportion in Human Development  | 45  |
| Five  | Conceptions of Time, Timing, and Times      | 55  |
| Six   | Writing Time and Timing Writing             | 69  |
| Seven | Concluding Time                             | 83  |
|       | References                                  | 95  |
|       | Name Index                                  | 105 |
|       | Subject Index                               | 109 |

# Preface

This book, as the title suggests, is primarily a study of the relationship between writing and the *kairos* construct, a construct linked in the classical Greek rhetorical texts to the production of oral discourse. *Kairos* has been the object of increased investigation among North American scholars of rhetoric and writing over the past twenty years or so. These investigations have often, although not exclusively of course, used *kairos* as a tool for the *post hoc* evaluation of written texts. Unfortunately, however, there has been little concomitant work that empirically or theoretically supports the "movement" of *kairos* from the oral to the written, or from production to analysis. The chief aim of this book, then, is to explore the bases for such support.

Much of the book is devoted to just such an exploration. However, if you'll pardon the poor paraphrase (and the poorer joke), a funny thing happened on the way to the Acropolis. That is, for example, in an attempt to provide at least one possible account of how an understanding of *kairos* (or, more specifically, an understanding of timing and proportion) might develop in individuals, a chapter was written to explore the overlaps between rhetoric, on the one hand, and cultural-historical psychology and cognitive psychology, on the other. Elsewhere, as I tried to account for how writers came to recognize a kairotic moment that was "externally" created, actor network theory was thrown into the mix.

The end result is that what was intended ultimately to be a rather straightforward study of *kairos* and writing became, instead, a multi-faceted examination of the construct. Which is a fancy way of saying that, although there's a fair amount of disciplinary ground covered, the coverage is more reconnaissance than invasion. As I discuss in several of the later chapters, this exploratory study does seem to offer possibilities for further research in such areas as writing pedagogy, context, genre, writing process models, and the development of expertise. Within each area, however, a further marshalling of troops and supplies (if I may continue with my military analogy) is necessary before any definitive conclusions can be reached.

Hunter Stephenson<br>
Houston, Texas<br>
October 27, 2004

1

## *Kairos*: Construct and Metaphor

In the opening of their article on the role of metaphor in the construction of knowledge and reasoning, Scholnick and Cookson (1994) note that they "have a fantasy of writing an intellectual history of psychology by examining changes in the meaning of its key concepts and terminology. It would trace how and why one concept was transformed into another and how and why a once popular concept disappeared and then suddenly resurfaced" (p. 109). If such an intellectual history of rhetoric were to be written, surely one of the key terms to be included would be *kairos*. *Kairos* has long been recognized by scholars of classical rhetoric as an important component of Greek and Roman rhetorical theories (e.g., see Cook, 1925; Untersteiner, 1954). Until fairly recently, however, *kairos* has received relatively little direct attention by classical rhetorical scholars in North America.[1] That situation changed somewhat with the 1986 publication of the chapter "*Kairos*: A Neglected Concept in Classical Rhetoric," in which the late James Kinneavy drew the attention of modern North American rhetorical scholars to the importance of *kairos* within the field of rhetoric and writing.[2] Kinneavy, like many students of rhetoric (e.g., Carter, 1988; B. Miller, 1987; C. Miller, 1992), sees *kairos* as comprised of two basic dimensions: "right timing" and "proper measure."[3] Given these two dimensions, *kairos* is distinguished from the other principal Greek construct for time: *kronos/chronos* (see, for example, the discussions in Barr, 1969; Dunmire, 2000; Jaques, 1982; B. Miller, 1987; Rämö, 1999, 2001). Unlike *kronos/chronos*, which refers principally to time as linear or "clock" time, *kairos* tends to be associated with experiential time and timeliness.

As is true with the English terms *time* and *timing*, *kronos/chronos* and *kairos* name abstractions that are perhaps best understood as theoretical or hypothetical constructs. *Kronos/chronos* and *kairos*, of course, cannot be directly apprehended through the senses, but they are hypothesized to exist because of certain sensible phenomena that are attributed as effects to them. In this respect, *kairos* is similar to, say, gravity or intelligence. The perception of Newton's apple falling from the tree to the ground does not provide sensible evidence of gravity itself, but rather provides sensual evidence for hypothesizing a force—which we call gravity—that operates on material bodies and causes them to behave in particular ways. Similarly, when we see a pedestrian successfully and safely crossing a busy street, we take that accomplishment as empirical evidence of the operation of intelligence, even though we cannot see, touch, feel, taste, or smell intelligence itself. Gravity, of course, is a scientific construct from the field of physics and intelligence a scientific construct from the field of psychology. *Kairos*, too, is a construct, but one typically associated exclusively with human discourse performance, even though the nature of the construct remains open to question.

Following Kinneavy's "call to arms," numerous scholars have focused their attention on the construct *kairos*. These scholars can be placed loosely into two groups. One group (e.g., Carter, 1988; Kinneavy, 1986; Kinneavy and Eskin, 1994; B. Miller, 1987; Rämö, 1999, 2001; Sheard, 1993; Sullivan, 1992) has reexamined the place of *kairos* in various classical and modern rhetorical systems. As it is treated in classical Greek rhetorical theory,[4] *kairos* is chiefly associated with oral discourse production. In contrast to the first group, a second group of scholars (e.g., Doheny-Farina, 1992; Dunmire, 2000; C. Miller, 1992) has applied the *kairos* construct to contemporary written discourse. That is to say, this second group of scholars has loosened *kairos* from its classical moorings in oral discourse production[5] and deployed it chiefly as a tool for written discourse analysis even as they use their analyses of completed texts to speculate about various aspects of production and the social conditions affecting production.

Notwithstanding the renewed interest in *kairos* on these two fronts, little work has been done that justifies either theoretically or empirically the "movement" of *kairos* from oral to written discourse. I intend to investigate how *kairos* might develop among writers and how they might come to construct or respond to a "kairotic moment," to use a now commonplace expression, during the production of printlinguistic texts. As I discuss more thoroughly later, an important question that seems to have remained thus far unasked and unanswered is whether *kairos*—which in rhetorical studies incorporates the principles of timing and proportion—emerges for individuals from similar principles that appear to govern human performance generally.

However, no scholar to my knowledge has investigated directly or empirically the twin possibilities that "*kairos*" for contemporary individuals is initially learned or acquired through activity in non-rhetorical areas of human performance and that what is thus learned in these other domains of human performance is then subsequently applied to the production and use of discourse. I intend to explore the possibility of ontogenetic origins for the principles of timing and proportion in human performance more generally and, if such origins can be identified, to investigate how "*kairos*" in general human performance might be transformed into a construct that figures in rhetorical performance. More specifically, this project focuses on the following three areas: (a) The ontogenetic origins of the principles of timing and proportion in human performance; (b) the subsequent transformation of these principles into the rhetorical construct *kairos*; and (c) the ways in which individuals understand and use *kairos* during the production and use of printlinguistic texts.

In order to better investigate each of these three areas, I developed the following primary research questions that I seek to answer in this project:

(1) Do the principles of timing and proportion govern human performance generally?

(2) Do "kairotic moments" occur in non-rhetorical or non-linguistic areas of human performance?

(3) Assuming that *kairos* originates in non-rhetorical or non-linguistic areas of human performance, how does it develop or transform into its rhetorical form?

(4) Can the relocation of *kairos* from its original oral tradition to a printlinguistic tradition be adequately supported (whether theoretically or empirically)?

(5) What, if any, understanding of *kairos* do writers have and how do they employ that understanding when writing?

(6) Based on the answers to the previous questions, do we (as researchers and rhetoricians) need to reconceptualize the construct of *kairos*? If so, how do we best do so?

Across the first three chapters of this volume, I discuss the *kairos* construct from several different perspectives. The remainder of Chapter One explores the early "history" of *kairos* as a word that appears in early Greek texts and its subsequent incorporation into both classical Greek and Roman rhetorical treatises. Chapter One concludes with a brief discussion of the metaphoric nature of *kairos*. Chapter Two extends the examination of the role of *kairos* in Greek and Roman rhetoric, focusing specifically on how the construct can be understood as both a symbolic tool and an independent force during the production of discourse. Chapter Three then considers how *kairos* is treated in other fields and disciplines, and how such treatments might contribute to the present study. Taken together, these three introductory chapters provide the background necessary for a detailed investigation into the three areas noted above. This more detailed investigation begins in Chapter Four which focuses on the ontogenetic origins of the principles of timing and proportion in human performance. In this chapter I explore two possible explanations for the development of these principles, explanations drawn from the domains of cultural-historical psychology and cognitive science/cognitive psychology respectively. The theoretical explorations which appear in Chapter Four are followed by two chapters which report on the three case studies I conducted as part of this study. More specifically, Chapter Five provides details on the study itself, including the study's setting and my methodology for both data collection and analysis. In this chapter I also introduce my coding categories and various data upon which the categories are based. Chapter Six contains a more detailed analysis of certain data, an analysis which expands and elaborates those coding categories first presented in Chapter Five. Finally, Chapter Seven presents a number of conclusions based on the previous six chapters as well as a brief discussion of possibilities for further research and several limitations of the present project.

## Tracing the Origins of *Kairos*

Posing questions about the origin and, hence, development of timing and proportion in human performance generally and human discourse performance specifically finds important support in Onians' (1951) etymological studies of the Greek word *kairos*. He initially suggests that the two meanings most commonly associated with *kairos*—namely, "right timing" (or "opportunity" for Onians) and "due measure"—are derived from two different roots. Onians traces the primary root back to archery: here, *kairos* denotes the moment in which an arrow may be fired with sufficient force to penetrate the target. The secondary root comes from the craft of weaving: here, *kairos* denotes the moment in which the shuttle could be passed through the threads on the loom.[6] These two definitions are strikingly similar and suggest, as Onians notes, that the two roots for *kairos* ultimately arose from a single source. Thus, White (1987), who draws heavily on Onians' discussion, concludes that "putting the two meanings together, one might understand *kairos* to refer to a passing instant when an opening appears which must be driven through with force if success is to be achieved" (p. 13).

Sipiora (2002a) argues that "*kairos* first appeared in the *Iliad*, where it denotes a *vital* or *lethal* place in the body . . . *kairos* thus, initially, carries a spatial meaning" (p. 2; emphasis in the original). This latter point is also made by Onians (1951) who points out that Homer used the term to describe a "place in the body where a weapon could easily penetrate to the life within" (p. 344). However, Onians continues, Homer did not use the term *kairos* or any of its derivatives to refer to "opportunity" or "due measure." Thus, Onians claims that based on this "early evidence we shall find reason to believe that [*kairos*] is not a mere abstraction" (p. 343). The use of *kairos* to refer to "right timing" and "due measure" is first found, according to both Onians and Sipiora, in the texts of the classic Greek poets Hesiod and Pindar. Sipiora (2002a) suggests that Hesiod is "probably the source of the maxim, 'Observe due measure and proportion [*kairos*] is best in all things'" (p. 2) from which, however, Onians (1951) argues that "little can be inferred" (p. 343) about the origins and meanings of the term *kairos*. What can be inferred, nonetheless, is that at least beginning with the works of Hesiod and Pindar, the term *kairos* carries not only a spatial meaning but a temporal meaning also and its connotation begins, as well, to shift from the literal to the metaphorical, from the concrete to the construct.

The earliest integration of *kairos* within a set of organized philosophical, religious, and epistemological beliefs is generally credited to Pythagoras and his followers. Drawing on earlier work by Rostagni (1922), Untersteiner (1954) suggests that *kairos*, the moment of harmony and balance, was a natural law for the Pythagoreans. Carter (1988), heavily influenced by Untersteiner, maintains that the Pythagoreans believed in a dualistic universe, a universe of agonistic elements wherein each pair of conflicting elements must be resolved eventually into a single, harmonious whole. The resolution of these conflicts relied on *kairos*. That is, *kairos* described the moment in time when the dyadic elements could be brought into harmony; *kairos*, encapsulating the notions of right timing and due measure, referred to balance. It was only after such a resolution, only after harmony or balance was achieved, that knowledge, belief and opinion could be realized or understood. As the time of and for conflict resolution, *kairos* helped to situate human affairs, allowing people to make judgments or decisions in a relativistic world.[7]

Carter (1988) also argues that for the Pythagoreans *kairos* referred to a "critical point in time and space" (p. 102) and, more significantly, that *kairos* "took on the more profound connotations of generation: the conflict and resolution of form and matter" (p. 102). Form and matter were, for the Pythagoreans, the basic or primary oppositional pairing. Form, the monad, emerged in the cosmos as a single point. The remainder of the cosmos (that which was not this point) constituted matter, the dyad. Using the monad and the dyad, the Pythagoreans were able to account for the creation of the remainder of the known (i.e., perceptible) universe. Certainly, as Carter suggests, *kairos* retained the spatial and temporal meanings commonly associated with the term within the Pythagorean system. However, while the temporal meaning remains relatively concrete in its connotation, the spatial meaning moves further towards the abstract. That is, although *kairos* as "time" refers to a specific moment in which resolution is achieved, *kairos* as "space" refers to an unspecified location (i.e., an indeterminate location within the universe) at which resolution is achieved.

Notwithstanding Carter's claim to the contrary, the importance of the spatial aspects of *kairos* appears to have declined in importance for the Pythagoreans, in as much as the spatial aspect referred to a concrete location (e.g., the archer's target or the space between the warp threads.) From this point on in its history, at least as a rhetorical construct, *kairos* is associated increasingly with its temporal aspect; its spatial aspect is increasingly ignored. In other words, the temporal aspect of *kairos* comes to dominate its spatial aspect: the "space" of *kairos* becomes the space in which the discursive performance occurs. It is, then, for much of the remainder of its rhetorical history, something akin to our contemporary concept "situational context," a point not lost on many modern scholars of rhetoric and writing (see, for example, Doheny-Farina, 1992; Kinneavy, 1986). Relatedly, translations of *kairos* as "due measure" are, in part, explained by the ascendancy of its temporal aspect. Onians (1951) suggests that because the archer's target and the weaver's warp present only limited openings that translations of *kairos* as "opportunity"[8] (i.e., the timing of the performative act) and as "due measure" (i.e., the force with which the act is completed) can be more easily understood. In either case, the available opening, though certainly bounded in part by spatial constraints, is largely limited by its temporal aspects.

Although *kairos*, which apparently names a construct, originates in early Greek thought and becomes a key element in Greek and later Roman rhetorical theories, it was often treated only indirectly. *Kairos*, as a rhetorical construct, was apparently rarely discussed specifically, unlike, for instance, the constructs *stasis*, *logos*, or *ethos*. Perhaps the most direct treatment of *kairos*, and the earliest treatment in a rhetorical treatise, was completed by the sophist Gorgias in his now lost "technical treatise on rhetoric," which may have been titled either "simply *Art* or possibly *On the Right Moment in Time (Peri Kairou)*" (Kerferd, 1981, p. 45; see also, Consigny, 2001). According to Kinneavy (1979), *kairos* was so important to Gorgias that he "centered his entire system of thought" (p. 306) around the construct and "had a situational epistemology, rhetoric, ethic, and esthetic" (p. 307) that were all based on *kairos*. Carter (1988) suggests that Gorgias answered the question "how, in a relativistic world, can a rhetor ethically choose among competing *logoi*?" (p. 103) through the use of *kairos*. In fact, Gorgias is credited by Dionysius as being the first rhetor to write about "the right time" although, Dionysius concludes, Gorgias had little of use to say (Freeman, 1949, p. 358; see also, Consigny, 2001, p. 43).

Although Gorgias' most direct treatment of *kairos* may have occurred in his lost treatise, he did explicitly reference the construct elsewhere in his extant texts. In his *Encomium of Helen*, for instance, Gorgias (trans. 1949a) writes when individuals "suddenly see fearful things they are frightened out of their immediate prudence for the immediate moment" (p. 80), suggesting that fear may preclude an understanding of the right moment for action (i.e., *kairos*). Elsewhere, Gorgias (trans. 1962) states that "the most divine and most generally applicable law [is] to say or keep silent, do or not do, the necessary thing at the necessary moment" (p. 130). Consigny (2001), drawing from Smith (1921), offers a partial translation of the same passage which states that the "most godlike and most common code" is appropriate action "at the fitting time" (p. 43.) In these two translations from Gorgias' *Funeral Oration*, the references to *kairos* focus largely on the proper act at the proper time. Once again, the temporal aspect of *kairos* overshadows its spatial aspect. While the temporal overshadows, it does not, perhaps, totally eclipse the spatial: a third translation renders the passage as "the most divine and universal law was to say and to stay and to commit and to omit the fitting thing in the fitting place" (Gorgias, *Funeral Oration*, trans. 1949b).[9]

However, the temporal aspect of *kairos* clearly dominates the translations of relevant passages from *The Defense of Palamedes*, one of the longest and most complete of the extant texts credited to Gorgias. For instance, Gorgias has Palamedes state "My judges, I wish to speak about myself to you and tell you something which may be invidious but is true; it would be unseemly if I were not accused, but since I am it is fitting" (trans. 1949c, p. 104). Palamedes concludes his passage of self-praise by claiming "But indeed it is not my own doing to praise myself; but the present time has forced me, and that when I am being accused, to make my defence (sic) in every way" (trans. 1949c, p. 105). In these two passages, as well as several others in *Palamedes*, the appropriateness of a discursive act is largely determined by its timing, i.e., by the temporal. However, Gorgias seems to suggest that appropriateness is also determined, at least in part, by place, i.e., by the spatial. That is, the presence of Palamedes at a specific location—before judges at a court of law—serves to justify the nature of the speech.

The temporal aspect of *kairos* is also highlighted in the work of Plato. For instance, Plato (trans. 1995) writes in the *Phaedrus* that the student of rhetoric becomes a rhetorician only when he has "a knowledge of the time for speaking and for keeping silence" (p. 553).[10] Despite various claims that *kairos* is a fundamental tenet within Plato's rhetorical system (see, e.g., Kinneavy, 1986; Sipiora's (2002) discussion of Levi (1924)), this quote from the *Phaedrus* appears to be Plato's only mention of the place of *kairos* within rhetoric. Elsewhere, Plato does connect *kairos* to his theories of aesthetics (see, e.g., Plato, trans. 1997) and virtue (Kinneavy, 1986). However, in Plato's most direct discussion of the role of *kairos* in rhetoric, the temporal aspect of *kairos* is clearly most important.

However, across many of Plato's works location implicitly impacts the appropriateness of discourse. More specifically, the place settings invoked by Plato in his dialogues appear linked to the dialogues' subjects or topics. For example, the discussion in *Euthyphro*, which takes place outside the courts, focuses on piety or pious conduct. The exchange in *Phaedrus* is ostensibly about love and lovers and occurs beneath a plane tree beside a brook. The dialogue in *Crito*, which takes place in a prison cell, is concerned with injustice and ethics. In *Phaedo*, which also takes place in prison, the conversation turns to human happiness, knowledge, and immortality of the soul. In these last two examples we see, if only implicitly again, a possible tension between the temporal and spatial aspects of *kairos*. *Crito* is set during the early days of Socrates' imprisonment; *Phaedo* near the time of his execution. Thus, in *Phaedo* the matters discussed are much more metaphysical (or religious if you will) in nature than those in *Crito* or, for that matter, any of the other dialogues. Seemingly then, in this dialogue, it is the place (the jail cell) and the time (only days before execution) acting in concert that determines the appropriateness of the discourse.

Aristotle, at least in relative terms, makes many more references to *kairos* than either Gorgias or Plato. In fact, as Kinneavy and Eskin (1994) note, "Aristotle's inclusion of kairos is not limited to its literal appearances, but is related to some of the main themes of the *Rhetoric*" (p. 433). However, for the purposes of the present discussion, I will focus on just the "literal appearances" of the construct, i.e., discussions of the construct and its place in rhetoric. One such literal appearance occurs during Aristotle's (trans. 1994) discussion of honor in Book I of the *Rhetoric*. He notes that "many obtain honour for things that appear trifling, but this depends upon place and time" (p. 53). Here, Aristotle differentiates between place (as *topoi*) and time (as *kairoi*) and, like Gorgias and Plato before him, foregrounds the temporal aspect of the *kairos* construct over the spatial. In a discussion on regaining the attention of the audience found in the third book of the *Rhetoric*, Aristotle suggests that "when the right moment (*kai-*

*ros*) comes" (p. 435) the rhetor must either stress the importance of the speech to the auditors or promise a new and wondrous tale. In this passage too, *kairos* chiefly refers to time (in the sense of timing or timeliness).

Roughly a contemporary of Aristotle and perhaps the best-known student of Gorgias, Isocrates also highlights the temporal aspect of *kairos*. For instance, in the *Antidosis* (trans. 1956a), Isocrates notes that although most of what he included was "written in the past," it was "inserted in the present discussion, not without reason nor without fitness, but with due appropriateness to the subject in hand" (p. 191). Past deeds, Isocrates states, are "an inheritance common to us all; but the ability to make proper use of them at the appropriate time, to conceive the right sentiments about them in each instance . . . is the peculiar gift of the wise" (*Panegyricus*, trans. 1961, p. 125). And finally, "fitness for the occasion, propriety of style, and originality of treatment" (p. 171), Isocrates writes in *Against the Sophists* (trans. 1956b), define good oratory. In all three of these passages, as elsewhere in his works, Isocrates uses *kairos* mainly to refer to temporal qualities.

As the "history" of rhetoric moves from the Greek to the Latin, *kairos* moves with it. However, *kairos* is not simply adopted by the Roman rhetoricians. Rather, it is merged with the Greek rhetorical concept *prepon*—the appropriate or fitting. Baumlin (2002) notes that although the "Latin *decorum* specifically translates the Greek *to prepon*, it would appear that Ciceronian theory combines *to prepon* and *to kairos*, 'the fitting' and 'the timely,' in a complex synthesis, at once observing both the formal and the temporal or situational aspects of discourse" (p. 143). In fact, writes Kinneavy (1986), "the concept of *kairos* merged with that of *prepon* (propriety or fitness) . . . [and] in this guise, *kairos* is the dominating concept in both Cicero's ethics and his rhetoric" (p. 82). Relatedly, but somewhat contradictory, Hughes (2002) argues that in the *Orator* Cicero "illustrates the subordination of *kairos* (as response to a specific situation) to appropriateness as embodied in the Aristotelian *prepon* and the Latin *decorum*" (p. 131). However, in his seminal work *The Sophists*, Untersteiner (1954) suggests that *prepon* is a "particular aspect" (p. 197) of *kairos* and first attributes the concept *prepon* to Gorgias (p. 198). Although the details differ somewhat, taken together these modern scholars demonstrate that the Greek rhetorical construct *kairos* was merged by later Roman rhetoricians with the Greek rhetorical concept *prepon* into the Latin *decorum*.

Perhaps even more so than *kairos*, the Latin *decorum*, most often translated as propriety, stresses the importance of the audience. The constituency of the audience plays a key role in determining the appropriateness of the discourse. This explicit link of *kairos/decorum* to the presence of the audience provides an implicit link between *kairos/decorum* and the material world. This line of reasoning suggests that *kairos* is important to not only rhetorical performance but human performance more generally. That is, *kairos* may figure into human performance in the material world. In any event, the importance of audience in the Latin conception of *decorum*, the "heir" to the Greek *kairos* and *to prepon*, suggests a subtle shift in the definition of *kairos/decorum*, a shift whose investigation is, unfortunately, outside the scope of the current project.

While it may not be entirely accurate, as Kinneavy (1986) once suggested, that "although the Ciceronian notion of propriety persisted throughout the medieval and Renaissance periods, the residual influence of *kairos* is almost a negligible chapter in the history of rhetoric since antiquity" (p. 82),[11] *kairos* has only of late undergone a revival amongst North American students of rhetoric and writing. These scholars have, with few exceptions, concentrated on the temporal aspects of *kairos* without discussing its original spatial aspects or, more importantly, questioning or exploring the ontological origins for individuals of the construct or its status. As I discuss below, I believe the status of *kairos* may be understood, at least in part, by viewing *kairos* as a metaphor. Such a view may also explain, again at least in part, why the temporal aspects of *kairos* came to dominate its spatial aspects.

## *Kairos* as Metaphor

The study of metaphor and its role in human ability to understand and explain the world is, of course, not new. As Ortony (1993) notes, "any serious study of metaphor is almost obliged to start with the works of Aristotle" (p. 3). Yet, at least according to Ortony, Aristotle considered the use of metaphors to be "primarily ornamental" (p. 3). Such a view on the role of metaphor contrasts starkly with the views held by such scholars as Lakoff, Johnson, and Turner. For instance, in *Metaphors We Live By*, Lakoff and Johnson (1980) suggest that "metaphor is pervasive in everyday life, not just in language but in thought and action. Our ordinary conceptual system, in terms of which we both think and act, is fundamentally metaphorical in nature" (p. 3). According to Lakoff and Johnson (1999) metaphors are so pervasive that "it is hard to think of a common subjective experience that is not conventionally conceptualized in terms of metaphor" (p. 45). Certainly, one such "subjective experience" is that of *time*.

Indeed, Lakoff and Johnson devote significant space to the analysis of metaphors on (or of) time. In *Metaphors We Live By* (1980), they identify three interrelated metaphors that are commonly used, at least in "modern industrialized societies" (p. 8), to conceptualize time: Time Is Money; Time Is A Limited Resource; and Time Is A Valuable Commodity (p. 8). These three metaphors are hierarchically arranged, such that Time Is Money is a subcategory of Time Is A Limited Resource which is, in turn, a subcategory of Time Is A Valuable Commodity. These metaphors are also discussed in their book *Philosophy in the Flesh* (1999). However, in this later work, Lakoff and Johnson introduce three additional metaphors on time: Time Orientation; Moving Time; and Moving Observer. These metaphors are based on the relationship of the observer (or speaker) to time, which, in these metaphors, is endowed with a physical presence. In the first of the three, Time Orientation, the future is in front of the observer, the present is co-located with the observer, and the past is behind the observer. In the second metaphor, the observer remains stationary while time moves; in the third, time remains stationary while the observer moves.

The nature or basis of these three metaphors lead Lakoff and Johnson (1999) to suggest that:

> Times (that is, time-defining events) are . . . conceptualized in terms of motion in space via the Moving Time and Moving Observer metaphorical mappings. Times are then conceptualized as locations or bounded regions in space or as objects or substances that move. Events are then located with respect to those locations in space or objects that move. Once this pairing of events with metaphorically conceptualized times occurs, the Event-for-Time metonymy can apply (p. 155).

Lakoff and Johnson maintain that the Event-for-Time metonymy allows individuals to refer to events by the temporal duration of that event. Events are thus bounded by their own beginnings and ends.

The philosopher John Searle (1993) argues that most, if not all, metaphors of time are spatial metaphors. That is, expressions like "the time flew by" or "the time dragged on" are not descriptions of the velocity of time. They are, instead, descriptions of sequential material states occurring in space. This point is also made by Akhundov (1986) who writes that "words designating spatial relations are used to express temporal relations, temporal prepositions are developed from spatial ones, and so on" (p. 22). The line of reasoning advanced by Searle and Akhundov is echoed in Lakoff and Johnson's (1999) statement (noted above) that an Event-for-Time metonymy occurs when "events are . . . located with respect to . . . locations in space" (p. 155). Searle's work also supports an earlier assertion put forth by Lakoff and Johnson (1980) that there also exists a Place-for-Event metonymy (p. 39), wherein a specific location stands for an event which occurred there. If in fact a Place-for-Event metonymy and an Event-for-Time metonymy both exist, simple combination yields a Place-for-Time metonymy. Indeed, the existence of this combinatory metonymy is supported by such expressions as "see you during class" and "let's talk at work." In such expressions the physical location stands for the time at which the speaker and/or the interlocutor will be at that location.

As I discussed earlier, *kairos* had both spatial and temporal aspects. That is, *kairos* referred to both a concrete location and a moment in time. Eventually, however, the spatial denotation was largely lost and *kairos* was associated almost exclusively with its temporal aspects. Given the work of Lakoff and Johnson (1980; 1999), Searle (1993), and Akhundov (1986) discussed immediately above, such a "change" in the definition (or at least the common usage) of *kairos* is understandable, if not expected. Although they were not discussing *kairos* directly, the arguments outlined by these scholars suggest that it is reasonable to assume that the temporal aspect of *kairos* developed from and ultimately subsumed the spatial aspect. The *kairos* construct commonly rendered as "right timing" or "opportune moment" or even "propriety" apparently entails the unspoken assumption that the "opportune moment" always occurs at or within a specific location.

On this view, *kairos* is a temporal metaphor that arose essentially out of a spatial metaphor. Imposing a view based on contemporary scholarship onto a 2500 year old term is not without risk of course. However, as Gurevich argues:

> We assume that the proper approach [for the study of the history of human thought] is to attempt to discover the basic universal categories without which culture is impossible and with which all its creations are permeated. These are at the same time the determinative categories of human consciousness. Here are meant such notions and forms of perception as time, space, change, cause, fate, number, the relationship of sensory to supersensory and of part to whole. (qtd. in Akhundov, 1986, p. 32.)

According to Gurevich, although the exact "meanings" of these categories change, the categories themselves are inherent to humans across their history.

Whitrow (1976) also suggests that time, at least as a phenomenological category, is a concept based in material reality if only because "the idea of time cannot be derived from prior concepts which involve no implicit appeal to it" (p. 525); thus "time must be regarded as ultimate" (p. 527). Unlike Gurevich, however, Whitrow suggests that the categories of time and space are not equally "determinative categories of human consciousness." Instead, Whitrow argues that "time is the basic variable rather than any spatial coordinate" (p. 526) because although "any object can be at the same place at two or more different times . . . it cannot be at the same time in two or more different places" (p. 526). Whitrow's assertion that the category of time is primary to that of space presents certain difficulties for Lakoff and Johnson (1980; 1999), Searle (1993), and Akhundov (1986) who argue collectively (as outlined above) that temporal metaphors develop from matters spatial.[12] However, of more immediate concern for my purposes here is that Whitrow provides further support for the contention that time is a universal concept. Ultimately then, given (a) the universal nature of the category *time* and (b) the profound influence of classical Greek scholarship on our Western culture, speculations on the metaphorical nature of the construct *kairos* seem, from this cramped perspective, rather reasonable and unlikely, to paraphrase Glick (1997), to (re)construct an historical term in order to "ventriloquate contemporary arguments" (p. v).

From its early uses until its adaptation and modification by various Roman rhetoricians, *kairos* has apparently been comprised of two distinct but related aspects: the temporal and the spatial. While it may be the case that the temporal aspect of kairos typically overshadows its spatial aspect, it is definitely the case that most modern scholars of rhetoric have ignored this latter aspect. While this criticism may seem rather summary in nature I believe that it is implicit across much of this chapter. This criticism will also appear, although somewhat more explicitly, in the latter part of the following chapter. In this next chapter I will examine more closely the role or function of *kairos*, especially within the classical Greek rhetorical systems and within contemporary studies of writing and rhetoric.

## Notes

1. This latter point finds support in the absence of even any mention of *kairos* in, for example, Kennedy's *Classical Rhetoric and Its Christian and Secular Tradition from Ancient to Modern Times* (1980) or Golden, Berquist, and Coleman's *The Rhetoric of Western Thought* (1976). Even more recently, and perhaps the more curious given its subject, there is no mention of *kairos* in Wardy's *The Birth of Rhetoric: Gorgias, Plato and their Successors* (1996). In contrast, there appears to be a long tradition of *kairos* study among German rhetorical scholars (see, for example, Bannerth, 1973; Boeckl, 1993; Pohlenz, 1933.) Additionally, *kairos* appears to have figured importantly in the work of many Western theologians including such notables as Paul Tillich (1967), Jean Daniélou (1953), and Oscar Cullman (1950). Moreover, *kairos* has apparently figured significantly in some research on psychoanalysis (see, for example, Ehrenwald, 1969; Hainline, 1980; Kelman, 1960.)

2. That Kinneavy should have called the attention of modern students of rhetoric in North America to the notion of *kairos* is, of course, no accident because Kinneavy's rediscovery of *kairos* as a rhetorical construct accompanied (in a kairotic way) his discovery of the origins of the Christian notion of faith in classical Greek rhetorical theory (see Kinneavy, 1987).

3. The word *kairos* is, of course, variously translated. These differences manifest themselves more often in the phrase "proper measure" which is also frequently rendered as "due measure" or "proportion." Although there may be some advantages to teasing out the differences in these translations, I am unsure what those advantages would be and, ultimately, what would be gained by such an attempt in terms of the present project. It is interesting to note that these, and similar, phrases have become the operating definitions of *kairos* within the field of rhetoric and writing, thus defining *kairos* by those phrases used to describe it.

4. Roman rhetoricians redefined the notion of *kairos* by deploying in its place the notion of *decorum* but I have been unable to find any applications among the Roman rhetoricians of *kairos* or *decorum* to writing or written texts.

5. It could, of course, be speculated that the classical Greek rhetoricians discovered *kairos* by "looking" backward from their memories of completed speeches to the production of the speech and that in this they were functioning in much the same way as when modern students of rhetoric apply the notion of *kairos* to completed written texts separated at least temporally from their contexts of production. As I subsequently point out, however, there is an alternative hypothesis, namely, that the Greek rhetoricians discovered in other arenas of human performance (e.g., weaving and archery) something akin to what they came to call *kairos* with respect to rhetors and oratory.

6. The conclusions Onians draws on these matters, which I discuss briefly here and in the second chapter, are supported by the relevant entries found in Liddell and Scott's (1846) *Greek-English Lexicon*. For instance, there are two separate entries for "kairos" in Liddell and Scott. The first, καιρός,, is associated with "a vital part of the body" (p. 689), while the second, καἰρος, indicates "threads, slips or thrums on the beam of the loom" (p. 689). Rather than integrate the work of Liddell and Scott with that of Onians, I have drawn nearly exclusively on Onians for the sake of improved readability.

7. On these matters, see, for example, Carter, 1988; Helsley, 1996; Kinneavy, 1986; and Untersteiner, 1954.

8. As Onians notes, the etymology of *opportunity* comes from the Latin *opportunus* and *opportunitas*. The original Latin root is *porta*, which, like its modern English equivalent *portal*, refers to an entrance or opening. However, despite such an etymology, the English *opportunity* is currently used to refer to matters temporal and not spatial.

9. Kennedy (1972), in his translation of fragments that originally appeared in the canonical work edited by Diels and Kranz (1951-1954), puts the passage as "the most godlike and universal law was this: in time of duty dutifully to speak and to leave unspoken, to act <and to leave undone>" (p. 49.) Thus, Kennedy (1972), as well as Consigny (2001) (who quotes Smith's 1921 translation) and Freeman (1949), stresses the temporal aspect of kairos, leaving the translation put forth by Hawthorne (1949) somewhat suspect.

10. This quote is drawn form a passage "spoken" by Socrates and so may further argument on whose views are actually represented in Plato's dialogues. However, I do not consider such arguments particularly germane to this project. I will note that the quote is the one generally used by classical rhetorical scholars when discussing the importance of *kairos* to Plato's conception of rhetoric.

11. See, for instance, the counter argument presented by Baumlin (2002).

12. However, Whitrow's contention that time is primary to space seems counterintuitive. He bases his claim on the fact that objects can only be in one place at a given time. Surely, however, if an object can be in one place at two different times, but not two places at the same time, then place is the more determinative factor. My concern with my lost keys is not based on when I left them but where.

2

## *Kairos*: Tool and Force

As I noted previously, *kairos* defies easy translation into English. This is due, in part, because there appears to be no single English term that encompasses the meanings generally assigned to *kairos*. *Kairos*, as a metaphor, subordinates its spatial aspect to its temporal aspect without, however, entirely losing its spatial grounding. Thus, it is difficult to properly translate *kairos* into English without losing one or the other of its metaphoric denotations. As it incorporates references to both time and space, *kairos* exhibits a dual nature. A second duality is also found in *kairos*: that is, it is described in both classical and contemporary rhetorical works as a tool to be used both for the production and the evaluation of discourse by either the orator/writer or the audience. However, as I will demonstrate later in this chapter, modern students of writing have employed *kairos* almost exclusively as a tool for evaluation.

Related to this second duality is another issue important to discussions of the ontological status of *kairos*, namely, (a) whether *kairos* exists or occurs independently of the rhetor and the discursive act, (b) whether *kairos* is "created" by the rhetor before and during the discursive act, or (c) whether some combination of the premises outlined in (a) and (b) act in concert and result in "kairos." At the heart of this issue is the question of "agency." That is, is *kairos* an entity (i.e., a "force") recognized by the rhetor and then acted upon or through or, alternatively, is *kairos* an entity that is created and then used by the rhetor. As attempts to separate my discussion of the status of *kairos* as tool from the status of the agency of *kairos* have resulted in a great deal of overlap, in what follows I will largely treat these two issues together, begging for the moment, for reasons that I hope will become clear later, a definition of the term *tool*.

### *Kairos*: Tool and Force in Early Greek Contexts

As noted in Chapter One, Onians (1951) has ably demonstrated that in some of its earliest uses *kairos* is associated with archery and weaving. In both contexts *kairos* refers, in part, to a location in space. In archery, *kairos* denotes the opening between two lines of targets. As such, it is external to the archer. In other words, the target exists independently of the actions of the archer. Although the archer may have, for example, put the target in place before the shot, the target is not created by the archer at the time of the shot. In weaving, *kairos* denotes the opening in the array of threads. However, this opening is not fully external to the weaver. It is, rather, fashioned by the weaver as she works the woof back and forth through the warp threads. In these contexts, the *kairos* is created through a complex interplay of the actions of the weaver, the configuration of the loom, the pattern of the weave, etc. It does not exist independently of the weaver nor is it entirely dependent on the weaver.

Notwithstanding my comments above on the creation of *kairos*, on at least one alternative view, the *kairos* of weaving could be considered to be more socially determined. The Russian psychologist A. N. Leont'ev (1981), in his *Problems of the Development of the Mind*, suggests that "for man a tool is not only an object with a certain external shape and certain mechanical properties . . . it [is] an object embodying socially developed ways of acting with it" (p. 296) and, in a similar vein, that a tool is "a social object, i.e. an object that has a certain mode of use developed socially in the course of collective labour and reinforced by [the] same" (p. 216). Tools (like the loom and woof of the weaver) reflect not only their current use, but their entire history of use and development. According to Leont'ev, human labor, like the tools developed and used as a result, also reflects its own social history. Essentially, then, if the work and the material implements (i.e., the tools) of the weaver are socially determined, then the result of their interactions—namely, the *kairos* (in the original sense of the opening in the threads)—should also be socially determined. Ultimately, however, applying Leont'ev's contentions as explanatory principles in this case yields a somewhat specious argument. Certainly, material objects created by humans encapsulate both their purpose and their developmental history. They lack, nonetheless, independent volition and agency. Only through their use, through their employment by the weaver, do the loom and the woof, despite the centuries of development they may each reflect, contribute to the creation of an opening, a *kairos*, in the threads. In other words, the *kairos* of weaving is not purely social in nature; rather it is created through the interactions of the individual and the material environment.

Both the *kairos* of archery and the *kairos* of weaving function, essentially, as tools for the production of good shots of the arrow and woof, respectively. The archer and the weaver must recognize the *kairos* (even as the weaver contributes to its creation) and take the appropriate action in order to ensure success. In one regard, then, there is a generative power associated with each *kairos*. *Kairos*, or at least its successful recognition, generates or induces the shots of the arrow and the woof. According to Onians, in its earliest uses *kairos* is associated with human performance although, importantly, not with human rhetorical performance. Such a claim is also supported by Liddell and Scott (1846) who note that *kairos* can be translated as, for example, "happening at the right place," "the *season* of action," and "to assist any one *at the right time*, hence in genl. to help, be useful to him" (pp. 688-689; emphasis in the original.) The etymological work of Onians and Liddell and Scott suggests that, in all likelihood, the (later) *kairos* of rhetorical and discursive performance developed from the (earlier) *kairos* of general human performance.

The Pythagoreans, for whom *kairos* was an important tenet, did not strictly associate the construct with rhetorical performance. Additionally, they are also credited with endowing *kairos* with more general productive powers. For example, in his essay "*Stasis* and *Kairos*," Carter (1988) suggests that for Pythagoras and his followers "*kairos* took on the more profound connotations of generation: the conflict and resolution of form and matter that initiated the creation of the universe and all that is therein" (p. 102). Carter draws heavily from Untersteiner's 1954 work *The Sophists* and it is worth quoting Untersteiner at some length, if only because he figures so prominently in later scholarship focused on, among other topics rhetorical, *kairos*.

> The philosophers of this school, if not Pythagoras himself, saw in *kairos* one of the laws of the universe, which were thus valid in general as well as in particular. *Kairos* and its allied concept *dikaion* [justice] "then found their application in the relations and communications between man and man, communications which are bound to vary according to age and office and kinship and state of mind."[1] This function of *kairos* has its roots in the Pythagorean doctrine of the opposites, which, bound together by harmony, give life to the universe. This form impressed on a logos or on its opposite is the work of *kairos* and the result is precisely *apate* [deception]. (pp. 110-111)

Certainly, the Pythagoreans believed that the original oppositional elements, namely the monad (form) and the dyad (matter), led to the creation of the perceptible universe.[2] It is not as certain, however, what role *kairos* played in this creation. Notwithstanding the claims set forth by Carter (1988) and Untersteiner (1954), there is little in the extant texts written or credited to various members of the Pythagoras school that points to such a dramatic role for *kairos*. Indeed, there are few references to *kairos* made by the Pythagorean writers, a paucity hinted at indirectly by Carter (1988, pp. 101-106) who cites none of the Pythagoreans.

In his book *Pythagoras and Early Pythagoreanism*, the Dutch classicist De Vogel (1966) also discusses the role of *kairos* within the Pythagorist system although he draws conclusions significantly different than those advanced by Untersteiner (1954) and Carter (1988). De Vogel relies on several references to *kairos* made by Iamblichus, a Neoplatonist scholar who wrote four speeches which set down various philosophical and epistemological tenets ascribed to Pythagoras and his followers. In his second speech, Iamblichus notes that Pythagoras "urged them to banish idleness from their actions; for there was no other good for every action than the right moment [*kairos*]" (as qtd. in De Vogel, p. 112). And, in a "remarkable final comment" (De Vogel, p. 116), Iamblichus writes that "up to a certain point the *kairos* can be learnt and it is not contrary to reason; it permits systematic treatment. However, in general and as such it has none of these characteristics. It goes together with and is, as it were, naturally bound up with the so-called 'right moment,' 'the fitting' and 'seemly,' and other such things" (as qtd. in De Vogel, p. 117). De Vogel's analysis of these references and the contexts in which they appear lead him to conclude that *kairos*, for Pythagoras, was synonymous with *circumstances* or "the modern term *situationism*, however with this restriction that for Pythagoras the 'situation' was morally and rationally determined" (p. 120; emphasis in the original). This "determination" was done by the individual (or the group) who judged the appropriateness of an act by evaluating the context in which the act was committed. Thus, as De Vogel points out, "even robbing temples and murdering one's next-of-kin" (p. 120) could, under the right circumstances, be "fitting." On such a view, an understanding of *kairos* becomes a tool for production, wherein production is looking forward to the proposed act. Assuming that circumstances do not change significantly, a proposed act may be judged against the relevant *kairos* and if it still seems appropriate, the act may be completed. If, on the other hand, the proposed act does not seem appropriate, it may be modified before its enactment or abandoned altogether. However, such a view also allows an understanding of *kairos* to be used as a tool for evaluation, wherein evaluation is looking backward after the completed act in order to judge its appropriateness. In both cases, kairos is linked to human cognitive planning. More specifically, using *kairos* as either a tool for production or a tool for evaluation implies that planning functions are an important component of *kairos* or, at least, an important component of the recognition of *kairos*. Although I will implicitly invoke this point over the remainder of this chapter and the next, I will not explore it in any detail until Chapter Four.

## *Kairos*: Tool and Force in Classical Greek Rhetoric

*Kairos* is first treated as a rhetorical construct in the works of the leading sophist Gorgias. Numerous scholars (see, for example, Carter, 1988, Kinneavy, 1986; Rostagni, 1922; Untersteiner, 1954) suggest a rather direct link between the *kairos* of the Pythagoreans and the *kairos* of Gorgias and the later sophists. Such an influence is disputed by De Vogel (1966) who argues that:

> For Pythagoras *kairos* is rooted in a cosmic-ontological order, whereas for Gorgias this background is completely absent. This makes for a radial difference; for it implies that for Pythagoras *kairos* had its place within a ταζις [order; system] and as such is of a rational-ethical character, whereas for Gorgias, where there is no such foundation, a complete irrationality remains. (p. 118)

While it may be the case that De Vogel overstates his position, he does agree that *kairos* figures significantly in the writings of Gorgias. According to Untersteiner (1954), not only does *kairos* have an "epistemological *motif*" (p. 196; emphasis in the original) within the theories of Gorgias, but when "translated into rhetorical terms, [*kairos*] becomes both capacity and precept" (p. 197). *Kairos* is first and foremost a capacity, by which Untersteiner means the ability to improvise and adapt speeches to the particularities of the time, place, and audience. Gorgias (trans. 1949c) addresses such an ability in several passages (quoted previously) from *The Defense of Palamedes*.[3] As he mounts his defense, Palamedes notes that he has included a particular topic in his speech (i.e., his self-praise) because it is appropriate given the situation in which he finds himself. In other words, he has adapted his speech based on the circumstances at hand. The ability to adapt the speech to the situation is also reflected in the remarks that close Palamedes' lengthy passage of self-praise.

These passages from *Palamedes* appear quite similar in that they suggest that the rhetor shapes his speech to best satisfy the time, place, audience, and purpose, in short, the context. Thus, in both passages, *kairos* has a tool-like function. That is, the rhetor can use his understanding of *kairos*, as he might use his knowledge of the issue or his prodigious vocabulary, to produce a better text. However, closer examination suggests that in the second passage (the concluding remarks) *kairos* cannot be considered a tool, even analogously, to be used by the rhetor. As a tool, *kairos* exists independently of the rhetor but lacks independent volition. In other words, the rhetor must understand or "read" the *kairos* in order for it to be useful during the production of texts. The first passage suggests, in fact, that Palamedes concluded, based on his understanding of the *kairos*, that is was "fitting" to incorporate self-praise in his defense. This contrasts significantly with the second passage wherein Palamedes states that he was "forced" by *kairos*, by the "present time," to include his lengthy self-praise. In this passage, not only is *kairos* independent of the rhetor, it seemingly forces the rhetor to produce certain kinds of texts, i.e., it exercises its own volition.

As I demonstrate later in this chapter and elsewhere, ambivalence about the nature and status of *kairos* pervades much of both the classical and contemporary scholarship. Inconsistency in the treatment of the construct is found not only across the works of different scholars but also, as seen above, within the work of a single scholar. The ambivalence seen in the passages drawn from Gorgias' *The Defense of Palamedes* illustrates the difficulties that arise when a single term describes, as Untersteiner (1954) suggests, both capability and precept, especially when these two roles are somewhat at odds. As a precept, *kairos* is one of many principles used to guide the rhetor in developing a fitting or appropriate speech. Untersteiner notes, however, that Gorgias "does not appear to dwell pedantically" (p. 197) on *kairos* as a precept. To do so would result in a tautology: establishing rules for the use of rhetoric would undermine the very situationalism that lies at the heart of Gorgias' rhetoric.[4] Yet, we could also read Palamedes' complaint that his speech production was forced by *kairos* as a complaint that the precept of *kairos* had forced his hand.

Such an interpretation finds some support in a passage from the *Funeral Oration*, where Gorgias (trans. 1962) suggests that the deceased (of which he spoke) "preferred mild reasonableness to harsh justice, often also correctness of speech to exactitude of law, holding that the most divine and most generally applicable law was to say or keep silent, do or not do, the necessary thing at the necessary moment" (p. 130). If *kairos* is a "law" or precept as Untersteiner suggests, then it is certainly a flexible one and meant only to guide individuals when choosing a course of action. Thus, it seems unlikely that we are to read Palamedes' complaint literally, for to do so would introduce the tautology noted above. However, if we read Palamedes' complaint figuratively, no tautology is introduced. Taken figuratively, Palamedes' complaint appears more as an apology, an apology for producing a speech that, although acceptable given the situation, was quite different from the standard or usual speech heard by the judges. Such a reading also reestablishes *kairos*, or at least its understanding, as a tool used by the rhetor. In other words, Palamedes was not "forced" by *kairos* to produce his lengthy passage of self-praise. Rather, he was "forced" by his understanding of the *kairos* of the moment to produce this passage in order to better defend himself.

Taken as a whole, Gorgias' treatment of *kairos* is fairly consistent within his system of situational rhetoric. As White (1994) notes, *kairos* was an essential part of Gorgias' rhetoric because he "imagines the activity of invention as the fortuitous falling together of a multiplicity of factors the issue or outcome of which cannot be foreseen" (p. 332). *Kairos* is, for Gorgias, a tool for production: the rhetor's understanding of the circumstances, the place, the time, help the rhetor produce an appropriate text. An understanding of *kairos* is also a tool used for evaluation, at least by the rhetor if not the audience. Palamedes, about to begin his lengthy passage of self-praise, implies that he has evaluated his as yet unspoken speech against the moment's *kairos* and found it appropriate: his planned speech would be "unseemly if [he] were not accused, but since [he is] it is fitting" (Gorgias, trans. 1949c, p. 104). There is, however, no clear instance in his various references to *kairos* that suggests that Gorgias considered the construct to be an evaluatory tool for use by the audience. Rather, it is the understanding of *kairos* on the part of the rhetor that is highlighted by Gorgias. Thus, even the "evaluation" of the speech is done by the rhetor *prior* to the actual discursive act. Occurring, as it does, before the speech act, the rhetor's self-evaluation is not a separate act of evaluation; it is, instead, a part of the larger activity of production.

Roughly a contemporary of Gorgias, Plato was opposed to the sophistic idea of a relative or situational rhetoric. Indeed, Kinneavy (1986) argues that although Plato intended his rhetoric to be an alternative to the sophistic system, *kairos* is central to both and further suggests that "in Plato's system, rhetorical thought becomes effective only at the moment of *kairos*" (p. 89). Likewise, Sipiora (2002b) contends that "Plato considered *kairos* to be a central element in any effective rhetoric, and the leader of the Academy was careful to define *kairos* with great care" (p. 117). Both Kinneavy and Sipiora base their claims on the oft-quoted (though differently translated) passage from Plato's (trans. 1995) *Phaedrus* wherein Socrates discusses the definition of rhetoric and a rhetorician:

> But when [the student of rhetoric] has learned to tell what sort of man is influenced by what sort of speech, and is able, if he comes upon such a man, to recognize him and to convince himself that this is the man and this now actually before him is the nature spoken of in a certain lecture, to which he must now make

a practical application of a certain kind of speech in a certain way to persuade his hearer to a certain action or belief—when he has acquired all this, and has added thereto a knowledge of the times [*kairos*] for speaking and for keeping silence, and has also distinguished the favourable occasions for brief speech or pitiful speech or intensity and all the classes of speech which he has learned, then, and not till then, will his art be fully and completely finished. (pp. 553, 555)[5]

The entirety of this passage leads Sipiora (2002b) to contend that Plato, speaking through Socrates, defines *kairos* as "the measurement of the discourse to the souls of the auditors" (p. 117). Certainly, Plato suggests that discourse must be "measured" against the audience: rhetoric is the "practical application" of particular types of speech to particular people to achieve particular effects. However, according to Plato it is only when the speaker has learned this practical application *as well as* "a knowledge of the times" appropriate for speaking that the speaker has become a rhetorician. Thus, Plato's rhetorician may, even after "measuring" the discourse against the interlocutor and finding the discourse appropriate, find that the moment, the *kairos*, is inopportune.

Notwithstanding one minor difference, both Kinneavy (1986) and Sipiora (2002b) render a key segment of this passage as "grasped the concept of propriety of time [*kairos*]—when to speak and when to hold his tongue [*eukairos* and *akairos*]" (p. 86 in Kinneavy; p. 117 in Sipiora).[6] Kinneavy (1986) suggests, prior to his discussion of the *Phaedrus* passage, that "sometimes *kairos* can be viewed as neutral and a 'good time' (*eukairos*), as opposed to a time without *kairos* (*akairos*)" (p. 85). The Greek words *eukairos* and *akairos* can also be translated as opportune or convenient and inopportune or untimely, respectively. All of these possible translations seem bound up within the instantiations of *kairos* (and its derivatives) in *Phaedrus*. Within the context of his dialogue, Plato uses *kairos* to denote "timing" and its derivatives to specify whether the timing is "good" or "bad." Most importantly, *kairos*, according to Plato, can be learned or, at least, a knowledge of it may be acquired, for it is only after such knowledge is gained that the orator becomes a rhetorician.

Within Plato's system *kairos* functions, to borrow Untersteiner's (1954) term, as a precept: *kairos* is a rule to be learned and applied by the rhetor.[7] Plato suggests that a knowledge of *kairos*, like knowledge of the types of souls and the kinds of speeches, can be acquired through instruction. Such a view of *kairos*, as an entity outside the rhetor with an almost physical presence (so much so that it can be "grasped"), accords well with Plato's epistemology. Less clear, however, is whether Plato considered *kairos*, again in Untersteiner's (1954) words, a capability or an ability to improvise and adapt speeches to the particularities of the time, place, and audience. Plato's passage in *Phaedrus* suggests that *kairos* does not play a role in determining the *logos* of the speech; rather, the *logos* of the speech is determined by analyzing the types of souls (i.e., men) present and then using those types of speeches learned theoretically to move those particular souls. Plato's *kairos* only becomes important after such analysis: *kairos* helps the rhetor decide whether to speak or keep silent; it does not help decide the content of the speech. Thus, Plato's conception of *kairos* also positions the construct as a tool for production, albeit a tool with a seemingly narrower application than in Gorgias' system.

Although a student of Plato, Aristotle advances a theory of rhetoric more relative than absolute (i.e., ideal); not surprisingly, Aristotle's conception of *kairos* often more closely follows a Gorgian model than a Platonic one. However, such is not the case in the few direct references that Aristotle makes to *kairos* as part of his rhetorical system. For example, Aristotle (trans. 1994) states that regaining the attention of the audience must be done "when the right moment (*kairos*) comes" (p. 435). Here, "the right moment" apparently not only has an existence but a force independent of the rhetor; the rhetor only needs to recognize the proper moment at which to reclaim his audience. *Kairos* is a precept and a limited tool for production. Elsewhere in his *Rhetoric*, Aristotle suggests that "many obtain honor for things that appear trifling, but this depends upon place and time (*kairos*)" (p. 53). Here too, Aristotle's *kairos* refers to a moment that exists (or will exist) independently of the rhetor and seemingly differs little from the *kairos* of Plato. Another direct reference to *kairos* occurs in his *Topica*, wherein Aristotle (trans. 1941) writes that "what happens at the right time (*kairos*) is called good" (p. 202). Again, Aristotle's treatment of *kairos* sounds suspiciously Platonic.

Aristotle's treatment is decidedly more Gorgian in those passages where he mentions *kairos* (or at least its derivatives) within the context of his own writing. In several places within the *Rhetoric*, Aristotle (trans. 1994) suggests that he has written enough on a particular subject given the situation at hand. For instance, in his delineation of the types of government, Aristotle claims he has addressed the matter satisfactorily "so far as was within the scope of the present occasion (*kairo*)" (p. 89). He limits his discussion of the subjects of deliberative rhetoric in a similar fashion, stating that "there is no need at present (*kairon*) to endeavor to enumerate" (p. 41) the topic further. The same term (in Greek) is used to end his examination of virtue and vice: "concerning virtue and vice in general and their separate parts, enough has been said for the moment (*kairon*)" (p. 93). Aristotle's comments resemble those made by Gorgias in *The Defense of Palamedes*, even as they form something of a "negative image." That is, Aristotle implies that his understanding of *kairos* has caused him to contract (i.e., cut short) his discursive activity. Palamedes, the Gorgian character on trial, implies that his understanding of *kairos* has caused him to expand his discursive activity. In these passages from Aristotle, we see then, like in various passages from Gorgias, that the rhetor's understanding of *kairos* functions as a tool for production. These passages from Aristotle also suggest that an understanding of *kairos* helps determine when speech should end as well as begin. Put another way, *kairos* functions as a tool for production from the beginning through the end of the rhetorical performance. Thus, as apparently conceived by Aristotle, a knowledge of *kairos* not only guides the rhetor in determining whether or not to speak, it also guides the rhetor in determining what, how, and for how long to speak.

Isocrates, a leading Sophist known to both Plato and Aristotle, also incorporated *kairos* as a fundamental tenet within his conception of rhetoric. However, as I will demonstrate below, unlike Plato, Aristotle, and even Gorgias, Isocrates is the first to place at least equal emphasis on the role of *kairos* as a tool for production and a tool for evaluation. Isocrates, then, appears to be the first ancient Greek thinker to explicitly link *kairos* with evaluation. For instance, in the *Panegyricus*, Isocrates (trans. 1961) suggests that "the deeds of the past are, indeed, an inheritance common to us all; but the ability to make proper use of them at the appropriate time (*kairo*), to conceive the right sentiments about them in each instance, and to set them forth in finished phrase, is the peculiar gift of the wise" (p. 125). Rhetors, then, can make use of knowledge shared by the audience but good (i.e., wise) rhetors will only make use of this knowledge when such use is situationally relevant. The worth of rhetors both good and bad can be determined or judged after the discursive act. Isocrates writes that "we should admire and honour" those rhetors who "are the most finished craftsmen" and "know how to speak as no one else could" (p. 125). Here, Isocrates links an understanding of *kairos* on the part of the audience, not the rhetor, as necessary for evaluating appropriateness. Clearly, audience evaluation can only occur after the discursive act; it occurs post-production. On this view, the act of evaluation "looks" backwards at the completed discursive performance even as it "looks" outward, situating that performance within the material world. Thus, as such an act of evaluation is based on an understanding of *kairos*, *kairos* serves to link rhetoric with the world.

This point is reinforced by Isocrates (trans. 1956b) in *Against the Sophists*, where he writes:

> What has been said by one speaker is not equally useful for the speaker who comes after him; on the contrary, he is accounted most skilled in this art who speaks in a manner worthy of his subject and yet is able to discover in it topics which are nowise the same as those used by others . . . [because] oratory is good only if it has the qualities of fitness for the occasion (*kairon*), propriety of style, and originality of treatment. (p. 171)

In this conception, the audience evaluates which orator best meets these guidelines; that is the orator who is "accounted most skilled." Yet, implicit in Isocrates' scheme is the ability of the rhetor to use his understanding of *kairos* to guide the production of his speech. In order to be successful, the rhetor internally compares his possible discourse against the requirements of good oratory (as outlined by Isocrates) which, significantly, vary with the situation. Thus, the rhetor's understanding of *kairos* aids in speech production; the audience's understanding in speech evaluation.

Isocrates also explicitly links an understanding of the moment with the production of discourse in *Against the Sophists*. Interestingly, this link is made when Isocrates specifically references his own writing, noting that "there is much, besides, of what I have written in the past, inserted in the present discussion, not without reason nor without fitness (*akairos*), but with due appropriateness to the subject in hand" (p. 191). Here, Isocrates uses *akairos* to denote, as Kinneavy (1986) put the matter, a "time without *kairos*" (p. 85) or, more specifically in this case, an inappropriate time for the introduction of particular texts (rendering, of course, the texts irrelevant.) Not only does Isocrates link *kairos* with his own textual production practices, he links an understanding of the construct with the production of written texts. Like Aristotle, Isocrates ties *kairos* to writing. However, it is difficult to infer too much (although tempting nonetheless) from this rather singular reference. Regardless, *kairos* does appear to be an extremely important construct in the rhetorical system envisioned by Isocrates.[8]

Yet, notwithstanding the passage noted above, Isocrates repeatedly ties *kairos* to the production and evaluation of oral, but not written, discourse. This is understandable, perhaps, given the function that oral discourse played in the courts, in the law, and in the "polite" society of classical Greece. Speeches may have been drafted (i.e., written) previously but they were still performed orally before an audience. Audiences listened to speeches; they did not read them. More importantly, audiences evaluated these speeches based on the *kairos* at the time of their performance, not the time of their inscription. Such evaluations were probably largely spontaneous in that they likely occurred during or just after the rhetor's discursive act. The audience would not have had copies of the speech available to them for later perusal and evaluation. Thus, although the audience's evaluation would have necessarily occurred post-production, there would have been little delay, hypothetically, between the receipt of a speech and its evaluation. Even so, a theoretical understanding of *kairos* as a tool for evaluation and production does not always lead to its practical application. For, as Isocrates (trans. 1956a) warns us in the *Antidosis*, even though we may understand *kairos*, we may find it difficult to use our understanding appropriately:

> For we are all so insatiable in discourse that while we prize due measure (*eukairian*) and affirm that there is nothing so precious, yet when we think that we have something of importance to say, we throw moderation to the winds, and go on adding point after point until little by little we involve ourselves in utter irrelevancies. (pp. 357, 359)

Human vanity, Isocrates implies, can override our sense of discursive propriety and, perhaps most importantly, create *akairos*, an inappropriate time, out of *kairos*, the right time.

If we take the treatises produced by Gorgias, Plato, Aristotle, and Isocrates as representative examples of the major, yet varied, rhetorical systems of Hellenic times, then it seems reasonable to assert that the construct *kairos* is an important tenet in classical Greek rhetoric. Although there are certain important differences in the treatments put forth by these four thinkers, there are also certain commonalities. Chief among these, for my purposes here, is that *kairos* or, more succinctly, an understanding of *kairos*, can be used by the rhetor for the production of discourse and by the audience for the evaluation of discourse. This dual role, of production and evaluation, although noted by some contemporary students of classical Greek rhetoric, has been largely ignored by modern researchers of writing. This latter group of scholars tends to focus on the evaluatory role of *kairos* at the expense of its role in production. Further, contemporary discourse analysts have failed to theorize adequately their appropriation of the *kairos* construct. That is, modern scholars use *kairos* as a retrospective, analytical tool in studies of printlinguistic texts without sufficiently justifying their transfer of the construct from its roots in oral discourse. These two points will be developed further in the following section.

## *Kairos*: Tool and Force in Contemporary Rhetorical Studies

Much of what I have written to this point has been, to some extent, historically bibliographic or, perhaps, bibliographically historical. Nonetheless, my previous text has introduced certain ideas and conceptions that will become more important in this section and across several of the following chapters. The first chapter and the first part of this chapter serve, following Swales (1981, 1984; Swales & Najjar, 1987), to establish the field, to demarcate and delineate, at least historically, the scope of concern. The remainder of this chapter, then, does perhaps even more vital work: it seeks to summarize previous contemporary research and, through that activity, demonstrate at least one research gap that may be filled by the present study. Accordingly, in this section, I will review several studies of writing and discourse by modern scholars who employ, to varying degrees, the *kairos* construct as an analytical tool. Further, as I noted above, I will highlight two specific problems with these studies: First, contemporary students of writing and rhetoric generally focus on the role of *kairos* in the evaluation of discourse, ignoring its role in the production of discourse. Second, these scholars have under theorized their application of *kairos*, a term rooted primarily in an oral tradition, to the analyses of printlinguistic texts. These two problems appear to be the result of what Courtney Cazden (1996), in her discussion of the proliferation of interpretations of Vygotsky, identifies and labels as "selective traditions." As I will attempt to demonstrate below, modern scholars have, by overemphasizing the role of *kairos* in evaluation, confused the part (evaluation) with the whole (*kairos*). Such a "selective tradition" is also evidenced in the failure of contemporary students of writing to draw on those specific passages of Aristotle and Isocrates that might authorize or lend credence to the use of *kairos* as a tool for the evaluation of written texts.

As noted previously, Kinneavy (1986) renewed scholarly attention in North America on the construct *kairos*. Not only does Kinneavy provide a succinct, yet expanded, definition of *kairos*, he also attempts to "reassert its importance for a contemporary theory of composition" (p. 80). Initially, Kinneavy provisionally defines *kairos* as "the right or opportune time to do something, or right measure in doing something" (p. 80). He then demonstrates that *kairos* is a multi-faceted construct with rhetorical, ethical, educational, epistemological, and aesthetic dimensions. Later, however, he equates *kairos* with the modern concept of situational context: those forces (political, social, material, etc.) that both constrain and enable a writer and the production of writing. It is this notion of *kairos*, as situational context, that Kinneavy uses throughout his discussion of a *kairos*-based college composition program.[9]

In his discussion, Kinneavy suggests that students should write on issues relevant to their majors and that their texts should be published. These suggestions are meant to connect students with issues that are important and relevant beyond the university because, as Kinneavy notes, "the academic can become . . . academic" (p. 101). Kinneavy's arguments are, in one sense, largely theoretical in nature and, as such, are fairly persuasive. What is missing, however, is any discussion of how students qua writers are to recognize the "right or opportune moment" for addressing such relevant issues or, indeed, how they are to recognize the "proper measure" within their own texts. The ability of students to recognize these elements appears crucial if *kairos* is to be the foundation for a composition program. This ability cannot be equated with the audience analysis schemes so often discussed in technical or business writing textbooks (cf., Lannon, 1997; Markel, 2001). Such schemes, while marginally addressing the issue of "proper measure," fail to discuss the other important dimension of *kairos*, namely, the "right or opportune moment." Unfortunately, Kinneavy does not delineate, at a practical level, how students are to recognize, or how they are to be taught to recognize, either the moment or the measure.

The student's ability to recognize the moment and the measure is also linked to a second problem in Kinneavy's proposal. As Kinneavy demonstrates, the concept of *kairos* is drawn from a culture that relied principally on orality in its discourse practices, particularly as those practices played out in the public fora of the *polis*. Within such a tradition, the rhetor and the audience were co-located, both in time and space. The rhetor was required to analyze *this* moment in order to determine what speech should be given to *this* audience. As many scholars have noted (e.g., Goody, 1977, 1986; Havelock, 1986; Kaufer & Carley, 1993; Ong, 1982), one of the principle differences between oral and written discourse is that the latter increases the distance in space and time between the rhetor and the audience. Thus, writing removes the writer (as the rhetor) from the immediacy of the audience and thereby requires the writer to analyze a future moment in order to determine what text should be produced. In a classroom setting, the writer can reasonably foresee when this moment will arrive; it will arrive generally on the date the assignment is due. However, this scenario does little, I would argue, to remove the "academic" from academic writing and, more importantly, it does not allow for the development of sophisticated, if any, understandings of *kairos* on the part of students.

The separation of writer from audience becomes an even more acute problem when writing for publication, especially when the writer has little or no control over when his text will be published. In such a setting, does the writer come to an understanding of the *kairos* at the time he actually authors the text? Or, alternatively, does the writer attempt to forecast the *kairos* of the time at which his text will appear in print and modify his text accordingly? Further, two features of writing, namely, its relative permanence and its wider dissemination (at least when compared to oral speech of classical antiquity) only complicate the ability of the writer to analyze adequately either the moment or the measure. Of course, the writer first needs to determine which moment needs to be analyzed or understood. Unfortunately, Kinneavy does not operationalize how *kairos* would function as a tool for the production of printlinguistic, as opposed to oral, texts and so leaves these as well as similar questions both unasked and unanswered.[10]

Like Kinneavy, Doheny-Farina (1992) fails to justify theoretically or empirically the transfer of *kairos* from the oral Greek tradition in which it was developed to the modern world of printlinguistic texts. This situation is exacerbated in that, to the extent that *kairos* was used as a tool for evaluation in classical Greek rhetoric, such evaluation was always linked to production. Here, Doheny-Farina has no immediate role in the production or the evaluation of the text in question; he is, instead, a somewhat displaced analyst with no vested interests in the text or the organization, interests that seem vital to determining appropriateness. In his article "The Individual, the Organization, and *Kairos*," Doheny-Farina discusses the difficulties college students face when moving from college composing to workplace writing, supporting his discussion with data drawn from a previous case study of a student writer interning at an abortion clinic. These data, along with a previous article written by Gates (1990), figure most prominently in Doheny-Farina's brief discussion of *kairos*. For, notwithstanding the inclusion of the word in the title, the article seems less centered on the *kairos* construct than on the concept of discourse community. That is, Doheny-Farina appears more concerned with how novice writers learn and adapt to the institutional standards of the discourse community in which they write, as those standards are used by the organizational members as standards for evaluation, not as tools for production.

Although Doheny-Farina initially defines *kairos* as "proper measure" and "right timing" (p. 293), he later, and quite extensively, uses *kairos* as a synonym for "situational context." In fact, the phrase "situational context" appears far more often than does the word "*kairos*." The effect of this substitution is to introduce the same problems that occur in Kinneavy's 1986 "*Kairos*: A Neglected Concept." For instance, Doheny-Farina (1992) fails to suggest how Anna, the subject of his case study, adapts her writing based on her understanding of *kairos*. In fact, Doheny-Farina implies that Anna has little or no understanding of *kairos* as she "had to subordinate her idiosyncratic view to one accepted by the members she dealt with" (p. 304). Originally, Anna produced a document that was unacceptable to her supervisors; she was forced to significantly revise her text, adopting and including more of the organization's "voice" than her own. As Doheny-Farina notes, "ultimately, Anna was quite unhappy with this trade-off" (p. 304); but, from my perspective, the "trade-off" was rhetorically necessary as it was required for the effective functioning of the organization that had hired Anna in the first place. Apparently, however, Anna grasped neither the proper measure nor the right timing of the situation and initially produced a text that was unacceptable.

Not only does Doheny-Farina leave unanalyzed the role of *kairos* as a tool for production in his comments on the novice writer Anna, he also fails to analyze the understandings of the components that may comprise *kairos* for Anna's supervisors. These supervisors were responsible for reviewing and approving the work done by Anna. Unfortunately, Doheny-Farina does not discuss how knowledge of either the "proper measure" or the "right timing" played a role, if any, in the evaluation of Anna's work by her supervisors. Further, Doheny-Farina also assumes that Anna and her supervisors held the same understanding of kairos and fails to consider how, if in fact they did, such differing conceptions may have contributed to the difficulties that Anna encountered. Rather, Doheny-Farina recasts the different expectations of Anna and her supervisors in terms of *ethos* or value systems/points of view. By recasting these differences Doheny-Farina significantly downplays the importance of *kairos* as a tool for evaluation and production, and, perhaps most telling, *kairos* is never linked to the actions of Anna's supervisors. Although he never raises the issue directly, Doheny-Farina's analysis of the actions of Anna and her supervisors subtly suggests that Anna, poor as her understanding of *kairos* might have been, was "understanding" a moment in time much more immediate than her supervisors. Anna, the intern, was perhaps mostly concerned with finishing the report and obtaining her supervisors' approval; her supervisors, however, viewed the report, which they considered an instructional document on how they waged war and won (p. 298), from a longer range, more historical perspective. Investigating such differential perspectives, their relations to understandings of *kairos*, and how such understandings impact the production and evaluation of printlinguistic texts seem central, indeed essential, to justifying the transfer of *kairos* from ancient Athens to the Western workplace.

The omission of any discussion on how or why the appropriation of *kairos* is possible or necessary is also evident in C. Miller's (1992) article entitled "*Kairos* in the Rhetoric of Science." That is, Miller skirts the issue of whether her appropriation of *kairos* as a tool for the evaluation of modern written discourse is theoretically or empirically justified. Here, too, Miller is cast as an analyst, one divorced from the relevant kairos and its linked roles of production and evaluation. Miller's unfortunate avoidance of a principal issue becomes increasingly noteworthy during her discussions of various temporal aspects surrounding the publication of papers on DNA by Avery in 1944 and Crick and Watson in 1953. For instance, Miller (1992) notes that Avery's article, which was poorly received, arrived at the *Journal of Experimental Medicine* three months before it was published; Crick and Watson's article, now a "canonical text" (p. 310) in molecular biology, arrived at *Nature* only three weeks before it was published. The time periods noted by Miller between article receipt and article publication are significant, if only because they suggest one of two possibilities particularly germane to this discussion.[11] First, a kairotic moment may be fairly durable over a period of time. That is, a given text, produced during a particular kairotic moment, may be published six months after it was written. If that text remains as "appropriate" at its publication as at its conception, that continued appropriateness suggests that the original kairotic moment spanned the six-month timeframe from production to print. Second, writers may be able to forecast or foresee the *kairos* of a future moment. In other words, writers may produce a text that will only become appropriate during a particular kairotic moment that will occur in the future.[12] Unfortunately, Miller does not analyze what impact either of these two possibilities may have on a rhetor's (or a writer's) ability to gain "a knowledge of the times for speaking and for keeping silence" (Plato, trans. 1995, p. 553).

Addressing the issue of temporal stability within kairotic moments is crucial to supporting, whether theoretically or empirically, the use of *kairos* as either a tool for the production or the evaluation of printlinguistic texts. If the construct of *kairos*, like that of gravity, remains constant over time and predictable, then individuals should be able to use their understanding of *kairos* to time and to measure their discourse. In other words, if *kairos* is durable, individuals should be able to forecast their discursive opportunities. Further, it seems reasonable to hypothesize that the ability to forecast such opportunities (i.e., the ability to recognize kairotic moments) requires certain levels of expertise and/or domain-specific knowledge as well as the application of various problem-solving skills. However, Miller (1992) fails to explore these lines of investigation, leaving unasked and unanswered questions that focus on temporal durability vis á vis *kairos*, on the ability of individuals to recognize such durability, and on the importance of expertise and problem-solving skills for such recognition.

Miller's (1992) work also exhibits another problem found in Doheny-Farina's (1992) essay. More specifically, Miller does not offer convincing evidence that *kairos*, a central concept in her article, played a significant role as a tool for production either for Avery or for the team of Watson and Crick. Although Miller certainly invites the inference that Avery had no understanding of *kairos* while Crick and Watson had a full understanding, Miller does not support her claim. Further, Miller does not demonstrate that an understanding of *kairos*, as a tool for evaluation, was employed by the relevant audiences in either 1944 (in Avery's case) or 1953 (in Crick and Watson's case) to judge the effectiveness of the texts produced. Rather, Miller herself, as analyst and rhetorician, uses *kairos* in an evaluatory capacity some half century after the events in question and looks backward from two completed rhetorical acts to the origin and production of those acts, making claims and inviting inferences about aspects of the authors' production activity all along the way, even though she never studied Avery or Crick and Watson directly.

Of course, Miller had no direct access to Avery, who died in 1955; nor apparently did she avail herself of any materials (i.e., letters, diaries, etc.) that might have provided textual evidence of Avery's thoughts around the time of his discoveries in the mid-1940s. As noted above, Miller invites the inference that Avery had little or no understanding of *kairos*, that his new knowledge required a new textual form. However, it seems equally plausible, especially given the lack of evidence, that Avery may have had a full understanding of *kairos*. That is, Avery may well have realized the implications of his discoveries but realized that the time was not right for their publication, regardless of their final textual form. In other words, Avery might have recognized that the time was, in Kinneavy's (1986) words, *akairos* or the wrong time. Such an inference, however, contradicts Miller's conception of the role of *kairos*. Miller (1992) suggests that "*kairos* teaches us some things about the complex nature of rhetorical context, or situation" (p. 323; emphasis in the original). *Kairos*, she continues, "also holds in productive suspension, the apparently objective and subjective dimensions of context, emphasized, respectively, by Bitzer and Vatz" (pp. 323-324). Miller's conception of *kairos*, which is rather Gorgian in its outlook, is only valid, however, under the circumstances implied by her conclusions on Avery's understanding of *kairos*. Other, and apparently equally valid, conclusions concerning Avery's understanding suggest that *kairos* is external to the rhetor, a much more Platonic outlook on the construct. Although several scholars of classical rhetoric have attended to the differences in the ways that *kairos* is treated across various rhetorical systems, these differences are largely overlooked by those contemporary scholars who employ *kairos* as a tool for evaluation. As B. Miller (1987) notes, the Platonic version of *kairos* dominates the scholarship, even where Gorgias is credited as the first rhetorician to have discussed the rhetorical construct (p. 173). The differences between the Platonic *kairos* and the Gorgian *kairos* are essential to understanding and appreciating the nature of the debate between Vatz (1973) and Bitzer (1968) wherein the former contends that rhetors create their own kairotic moments (i.e., the Gorgian version) and the latter maintains that kairotic moments are independent of the rhetor (i.e., the Platonic version).

Notwithstanding such definitional issues, C. Miller (1992), along with Kinneavy (1986) and Doheny-Farina (1992), begs the question of *kairos* as a tool for production. Perhaps more importantly, they also beg the question of the origins of *kairos* as a principle governing human performance. Indeed, they provide no evidence to suggest that *kairos* is any thing other than epiphenomenal in nature and fail to question or explore its ontogenetic origins. Regardless of its domain (e.g., baseball, molecular biology, medicine), human performance, or at least successful human performance, would appear always to be in some sense kairotic in nature in that such performance is dependent on timing and proportion. Do, in fact, the principles of timing and proportion—which likely govern successful human performance generally—become transformed and modified into the construct of *kairos* as individuals develop their capacities as rhetors? And, assuming for the moment such transformation and modification, can the appropriation of *kairos* from its roots in the oral Greek rhetorical tradition for the analysis of written texts be theoretically justified? It seems reasonable, at this stage, to regard these two questions as empirical ones. The remainder of this project will seek to answer them.

## Notes

1. Although Untersteiner does not credit this quotation directly, based on the surrounding text he appears to have drawn it from Rostagni (1922).

2. On these matters see Freeman, 1949 and O'Meara, 1989 as well as Carter, 1988 and Untersteiner, 1954.

3. The two relevant quotes are "my judges, I wish to speak about myself to you and tell you something which may be invidious but is true; it would be unseemly if I were not accused, but since I am it is fitting" (p. 104) and "but indeed it is not my own doing to praise myself; but the present time has forced me, and that when I am being accused, to make my defence (sic) in every way" (p. 105).

4. Avoiding this tautology may help explain why Gorgias was both credited and criticized by Dionysius. Dionysius writes that Gorgias was the first to write about "the right time" but complains that he had little useful to say on the topic. On these matters, see, for example, Consigny (2001, p. 43) and Freeman (1949, p. 358).

5. Kinneavy (1986) utilizes a translation of *Phaedrus* by Helmbold and Rabinowitz (1958) who render the phrase "a knowledge of the times" as "grasped the concept of propriety of time" (pp.271-272). Curiously, although he includes a translation of the passage that matches the one appearing in Kinneavy (1986), Sipiora (2002b) cites the same translation of *Phaedrus* from which the passage above is drawn.

6. The translation cited by Sipiora (2002b) omits "concept of" from the phrase.

7. However, it is unclear from Untersteiner's assessment whether such rules (i.e., precepts) are learned through instruction or by observation of human behavior. Understanding how *kairos* is learned seems vital to implementing, as Kinneavy (1986) advocates, a *kairos*-based composition program. See Spradley's (1972) introductory chapter (and especially pp. 18-35) for a discussion on rules, their origins, and their features.

8. The construct also figures prominently in his views on ethics, politics, and jurisprudence (see, e.g., the discussion in Sipiora, 2002a).

9. It is worth noting that Kinneavy based his program on the productive aspect of *kairos*, an aspect largely ignored by later rhetorical scholars.

10. Kinneavy also fails to consider differences that obtain between writing in the composition classroom and the workplace. Chiefly, he fails to account for why texts are created in the workplace or how imposed deadlines affect such creation. Kinneavy, apparently assuming that composition instruction can overcome the distances between composition and workplace writing, ignores the possibility that *kairos* might function differently in the two settings. Further, with few exceptions, students understand that the instructor is always the final audience and arbiter, regardless of the set-up of the writing course.

11. There may, of course, have been other reasons for the differences in the times between article receipt and publication. For instance, the mechanics of publication may have improved between 1944 and 1953 or the materials necessary for publication may have not been as readily available in 1944 during the height of World War II. Neither of these possibilities is noted by Miller.

12. The possibility exists that the kairotic moment in place at the time of production "disappeared" only to occur again at the time of publication. Such an event seems unlikely but would also require the writer to forecast the reoccurrence of the original kairotic moment. In this regard, this third possibility differs little in its essentials from the second possibility discussed in the text proper.

3

## *Kairos* Outside The Domain Of Rhetoric

As I discussed in previous chapters, Onians (1951) has demonstrated that *kairos* is associated, etymologically and probably in its origins, with archery and weaving. As such, *kairos* is linked historically with at least two areas of human performance prior to rhetoric. In this chapter I seek to extend, in a way, Onians' work. This extension is based on the assumption that a valid and worthwhile possibility for better understanding the role of *kairos* in human performance is to investigate how the construct is defined and deployed in fields and disciplines other than rhetoric. Thus, in what follows, I explore how *kairos* figures in the works of several scholars whose primary interests lie outside the study of writing and rhetoric. My exploration is, of course, as Clifford (1986) puts it, "inherently partial—committed and incomplete" (p. 7). Committed in that what follows reflects my own biases, acknowledged or not, and incomplete in that what follows is not an exhaustive survey of the extant literature. Notwithstanding these flaws—which, according to Clifford, can never be eliminated entirely anyway—I maintain that this review will prove profitable.

### *Kairos* and historical analysis

John E. Smith, a scholar working at the intersections of philosophy, history, and religion, first discussed *kairos* in a 1969 article entitled "Time, Times, and the 'Right Time': *Chronos* and *Kairos*." In 1986, he revisited his earlier treatment of *kairos*, in part due to the influence of Kinneavy's (1986) "*Kairos*: A Neglected Concept in Classical Rhetoric." Smith writes, in 1986, that although he was aware that *kairos* had "metaphysical, historical, ethical, and esthetic applications" (p. 3), he was unaware that *kairos* also had rhetorical applications. He also notes, in his later piece, that scholars of both rhetoric and philosophy have "neglected" *kairos*, a point made earlier in this volume. Smith (1986) suggests that such neglect is "unfortunate" as *kairos* "expresses a most important feature of temporal process which, despite exceptions here and there, is not expressed in the concept of *chronos*" (p. 3). As C. Miller (1992) notes, in a rare use by a student of rhetoric of scholarship on *kairos* from outside the field, Smith associates *chronos* with quantitative time and *kairos* with qualitative time.

Smith's bifurcation of time into a quantitative *chronos* and a qualitative *kairos* is, of course, a fairly standard treatment. Dunmire (2000), for instance, in her discussion of the relations obtained between temporality and genre activity, posits a division between "process time" (i.e., kairotic or qualitative time) and "clock time" (i.e., chronotic or quantitative time), a division she draws from Davies (1990). Smith (1969), however, does not suggest that *chronos* and *kairos* are "utterly distinct" (p. 2). Rather, Smith argues that "*kairos* presupposes *chronos* and is therefore a necessary condition for history and historical knowledge, but that by itself *chronos* does not suffice for the sort of historical interpretation in which we commonly engage" (p. 2). In other words, an understanding of quantitative time can not, by itself, help us grasp the importance of particular events; what is needed is an understanding of qualitative time. As Prince (1978) points out, "history is less concerned with predictable, recurrent events than with singular incidents" (p. 17). And, in order to properly interpret these singular points in history, an understanding of *kairos* is needed.

In his 1986 article, although he does again address the importance of *kairos* for the study and interpretation of history, Smith's discussion of the construct is somewhat broader and draws from a wider range of sources. Motivated in part, perhaps, by the desire to not lose *kairos* to the rhetoricians following Kinneavy's (1986) "Neglected Concept" article, Smith attempts to clearly differentiate the *kairos* of history from that of rhetoric. Smith (1986) writes that:

> It is important to notice at this point that the understanding of *kairos* within the scope of rhetoric primarily tended toward an emphasis, if not an over-emphasis, on human action since rhetoric is an art or skill concerned with communication and persuasion. This emphasis, however, must not be allowed to overshadow the ontological dimension of *kairos* as manifest in various orders of happening, such as constellations of historical events, natural processes and developments which have their own temporal frames and opportune times quite apart from human action, especially the action of this or that individual. (p. 5)

Pointing to the actions of the vintner, whose determination of the "right time" to pick the grapes is almost entirely dependent on environmental factors, Smith suggests that although the "right time"—the "when" to pick the grapes—will always be based on an individual's judgment, although such judgment "does not create that 'when' out of itself" (p. 6). In other words, the individual does not create *kairos*; instead the individual reads or interprets various cues from the material environment and comes to an understanding of *kairos*. *Kairos*, for Smith, apparently exists independently of the individual.

Smith's conception of *kairos* is also linked with production. For Smith, understanding *kairos* enables individuals to discern the right time for action; an individual can use this understanding to guide her production of performative behaviors. Although Smith argues for a version of *kairos* similar to that advanced by Plato, Smith is otherwise decidedly "anti-rhetorical" in his stance. For instance, Smith (1986) argues that:

> The time of *kairos* is seen as an ontological element in the basic structure of things and, while that time calls for a human response, the occasion itself is not of human devising. I stress the point in order to counteract the idea that, as might appear from the context of rhetoric, *kairos* represents no more than a human standpoint. That interpretation is ruled out because of the clearly metaphysical context of the statements in question. (p. 13)

The "statements in question" are various passages written by Plato in the fourth book of the *Laws*, one of three Platonic works that Smith cites.[1] Thus, while he acknowledges the scholarly debt owed to rhetoric generally and Kinneavy specifically, Smith clearly seeks to broaden the application of the construct.

Smith's interest in the productive aspects of *kairos* is counter-balanced by his interest in its evaluative aspects. Notwithstanding his definitional work on *kairos*, Smith (1969) is more interested in "[determining] the role of each [i.e., *kairos* and *chronos*] in expressing the historical dimension of reality" (p. 2). In his later article, Smith (1986) writes that "occasions are times which must be apprehended as such through historical insight; they are, moreover, times for historical decision and action" (p. 13). This stress upon matters "historical" clearly positions an understanding of *kairos* as a tool to be used by the historian for analysis or evaluation. In other words, the historian's ability to separate the important moments (i.e., Smith's times of *kairos*) from those mundane is what distinguishes history from chronicle (see, e.g., Smith, 1986, p. 10). In this regard, Smith points out that a particular kairotic moment has an ordinal position that distinguishes it from the background chronology. Apparently, however, given Smith's failure to demonstrate how such an ordinal position can be determined in advance, such a distinction can only be verified after the fact, i.e., after the event in question.

Such a distinction also requires human intervention. The importance of a particular occasion can only be determined by evaluating it against those occasions which came immediately before or which followed immediately after. As humans conduct such evaluations, it is unclear how, although Smith (1986) argues against the position, that *kairos* can "represent" anything other than a "human standpoint" (p. 13). This is not to suggest that *kairos* is, or can be, created through rhetorical action (i.e., language) alone. On this matter, I believe that Smith is correct when he states that kairotic moments are not entirely human linguistic inventions. What I am trying to suggest, however, is that *kairos* can not exist entirely independently of humans. The determination of the "right time" is a determination made by humans; it is the result of a human cognitive action. Certainly, the vintner's decision regarding the "right time" in the maturation cycle of wine is dependent on various natural processes which would occur regardless of the presence of humans. Still, the vintner's decision is a *human* decision bound by forces both material (e.g., the aging cycle) and social (e.g., wine drinkers prize this taste or this color in wine.) And, of course, grapes do not end up, peeled and pulped, in wine vats of their own accord. Grapes become wine, whether Mad Dog 20-20 or Lafitte Rothschild, because of human activity. Nonetheless, implicit in Smith's work is the argument that human activity is not synonymous with human discourse and that *kairos* is not created entirely by the latter.

Smith (1986) attributes "three distinct but related concepts" (p. 10) to *kairos*, each of which points to the importance of human activity as a defining characteristic of the construct. First, *kairos* is "right timing." Second, *kairos* "means a time of tension and conflict . . . that calls for a decision at *that* time" (p. 10; emphasis in the original). And third, *kairos* "means that the problem or crisis has brought with it a time of opportunity . . . for accomplishing some purpose which could not be carried out at some other time" (pp. 10-11). Smith argues that "implicit in all three meanings embraced by *kairos* is the concept of an *individual* time having a critical ordinal position set apart from its predecessors and successors" (p. 11; emphasis in the original). Here too, however, the criticality of a particular "individual time" can only be determined by humans and, perhaps most importantly, can only be determined after the fact.

Although Smith does an admirable job of demonstrating that *kairos* has broader applications than those generally ascribed to it by scholars of rhetoric, he falls victim to some of the same pitfalls previously encountered by said scholars. That is, chiefly, Smith stresses the productive aspects of *kairos* but does not specify how such aspects develop in humans or function in their general performance. He falls back, then, as many rhetoricians have done, on the analytic and evaluative aspects of the construct, aspects much easier to specify, if only because *post hoc* analysis lends itself to such specification. Indeed, his integration of *kairos* as a tool for the analysis of historical events fails, ultimately, to establish concretely if the human participants in a given event recognized the time as the "right time" before the event unfolded.

## *Kairos* and Christian theology

Similar conceptions of *kairos*, as a means for understanding the importance of particular events as they manifest themselves across historical time, can also be found in the work of numerous Western Christian theologians, including Jean Danièlou (1953), Oscar Cullman (1950), and Paul Tillich (1967). The latter scholar's work may be most important here, if only because Kinneavy "first encountered the term *kairos* while reading Paul Tillich and was intrigued by the possibilities of interpretation that the term might offer a rhetorician" (Thompson, 2002, p. 196). Presumably, Kinneavy was reading Tillich's work as part of his then ongoing research, research that ultimately culminated in his 1987 volume entitled *Greek Rhetorical Origins of Christian Faith: An Inquiry*. In any case, although *kairos* had fallen out of favor among rhetoricians, it remained a viable and important construct for many theologians.[2]

The importance of *kairos* in Christian theology is due, in part, to the various political and social forces that led to a New Testament written in Greek. As a result, contemporary theologians and rhetoricians are largely dealing with the same term; however, unlike their counterparts in rhetoric, religious scholars seem unconcerned with the etymology and uses of *kairos* prior to the New Testament. Still, this is not meant to imply that they are unmindful of the various ways in which *kairos* can be or was translated in the New Testament. Tillich (1967) associates *kairos* with the "fulfillment of time" (Vol III, p. 369). Expanding on this definition, Tillich writes that:

> Its original meaning—the right time, the time in which something can be done—must be contrasted with *chronos*, measured time or clock time. The former is qualitative, the latter quantitative. In the English word "timing," something of the qualitative character of time is expressed, and if one would speak of God's "timing" in his providential activity, this term would come near to the meaning of *kairos*. (Vol III, p. 369)

Tillich's division of time into a qualitative kairotic time and a quantitative chronotic time echoes the temporal division advanced by Smith (1969; 1986) discussed previously. However, Tillich's conception of history (as well as Cullman's and Danièlou's) differs sharply from Smith's. Smith looks "backwards" across the chronology of completed events, analyzing and evaluating previously completed events. Tillich, on the other hand, holds an eschatological view of history, a view that looks "forward" across time to the Second Coming of Christ.

Tillich's definition of *kairos* is also informative as it points to the distinction he draws between a secular and a religious *kairos*. This distinction is echoed by Cullman (1950) who writes that "*kairos* in secular usage is the moment in time which is especially favorable for an undertaking . . . it is human considerations that cause a point of time to appear" advantageous (p. 39). Religious *kairos*, on the other hand, relies not on decisions made by humans but on the decision of God. Both Tillich and Cullman maintain that there is one great religious *kairos*, one ultimate "time of fulfillment": namely, the second coming of Christ. This final *kairos*, the time of which is unknown to all but God, is punctuated by *kairoi* which Tillich (1967) suggests are "continually recurring and derivative" of the *kairos* and account for those moments "in which a religious cultural group has an existential encounter" (Vol III, p. 153) with the Holy Spirit. In a similar vein, Cullman (1950) writes that "God fixes these *kairoi* in the context of his entire plan of salvation" (p. 40); *kairoi* are redemptive occasions in the history of humans. For both Tillich and Cullman, the creation of a kairotic moment is a divine act. Although humans cannot create *kairos*, they can have knowledge of the importance of such moments. Such knowledge is gained through religious or ecstatic visions (Tillich, 1967, Vol III, p. 370) or by comparing the present occasion with "the past *kairos*" (Cullman, 1950, p. 42). Only past or ongoing *kairoi* can be known to humans. Both Cullman and Tillich explicitly state that humans have no knowledge of future *kairoi* which, like the final *kairos*, are known only to God. Tillich suggests that "foresight [of a *kairos*] in any scientific-technical sense is impossible" (Vol III, p. 371). He further contends that *kairos* "is not an object of analysis and calculation such as could be given in psychological or sociological terms" (Vol III, p. 370).

The use of a past *kairoi* to understand present or future *kairoi* is an analytical activity related to Christian typology. Especially early in the history of Christianity, various religious thinkers attempted to link the theology of the Old Testament with the theology of the New Testament. Such links were often forged by highlighting certain characteristics of an event from the Old Testament and then weaving those characteristics into events depicted in the New Testament and the liturgies of the Christian churches. For example, during the Great Flood of the Old Testament, eight members of Noah's family (including Noah of course) were saved, protected in the Ark. The number 8 figures significantly in later Christian practices. Baptism founts, for instance, are generally eight-sided; the renewal of baptism promises a new day, the new day being the eighth day, the first day after the initial creation cycle. The Great Flood can be considered kairotic in nature; in Tillich's and Cullman's terms, the event was a *kairoi*: a time wherein a part of God's plan became known to humans. An understanding of individual *kairoi*—which links events past to those present and foreshadow those to come—assists in the management of human faith, in as much as faith guides the converted in the conduct of their lives. There are then, within Western Christian theology, productive and performative aspects to *kairoi* and *kairos*.

The conceptions of *kairos* advanced by Tillich and Cullman are fairly similar to each other: both scholars suggest that humans experience kairotic moments, that humans understand these moments to be important, and that humans can not forecast the occurrence of these moments. The view of *kairos* shared by Tillich and Cullman is similar, in at least one respect, to the general view of the construct held by students of rhetoric: namely, that humans become cognizant that "this moment" would be an advantageous one for the conduct of their affairs. Within the discipline of rhetoric, of course, such affairs include generally only the production of oral discourse (in classical contexts) or the production and evaluation of written discourse (in contemporary contexts.) Within the works of these theologians there are, of course, no such delimitations: kairotic moments occur during and across a broad spectrum of human affairs, even as those moments are a part of God's larger plan. Thus, the work of Tillich and Cullman, broadly conceived, can be said to demonstrate, at least implicitly, the importance of the construct of *kairos* in characterizing human performance.

## *Kairos* and psychoanalysis

Like its role in Western Christian theology, the *kairos* of psychoanalysis serves as a linguistic descriptor. Within the field of psychoanalysis, *kairos* points to those moments during an individual's lifespan in which various "breakthroughs" are achieved. Thus, while the *kairos* of both theology and psychoanalysis is concerned with singular events, the *kairos* of psychoanalysis focuses on those events that unfold in a particular person's history and not, as with theology, on those events that unfold across history more generally. On at least one account, the *kairos* construct was only fairly recently incorporated into the field. According to Kelman (1969), it was only "in 1956 [that] Kielholz introduced the concept of *kairos* into psychotherapy" (p. 62). This claim is supported by Goldwert (1991) who contends that "it was the existential psychotherapist, Arthur Kielholz, who revived and channeled Hippocratic *Kairos* into psychotherapy" (p. 553). Notwithstanding his own intellectual debt, Kelman (1969; see also Kelman, 1960) has also apparently been very influential and is cited heavily by Hainline (1980) and, to a lesser extent, Goldwert (1991).

Not surprisingly, such scholars as Kelman, Hainline, and Goldwert do not trace *kairos* back to the classical Greek rhetoricians. Rather, they locate the origins of the term in Greek mythology where Kairos, the son of Zeus, was the god of opportunity. The god Kairos, suggests Hainline (1980), "symbolizes eternal time, archetypal time which cannot be measured by the quartz chronometer to which modern Western man is bound" (p. 325). Kelman (1969), who works from the same mythological source, contends that *kairos* "implies a right time in the course of events to do certain things that will favor a crucial happening; the necessity to be aware that there is such a right time so that it might be prepared for; and that it is an opportunity which must be immediately recognized and seized upon" (p. 80). Although Kelman was defining *kairos* in terms of its applications within psychotherapy, Goldwert (1991) is even more specific about the role of the construct. Goldwert maintains that *kairos* denotes those "specific times in therapy when a patient is psychically prepared for a specific kind of intervention and the success, at that moment, is assured, when it would have been premature before or without prospects after" (pp. 553-554). Kelman (1969) is quick to point out, however, that not all therapeutic "cures" are kairotic in nature (p. 64). Rather, he argues that *kairos*, as a breakthrough moment in analysis, only occurs when different alternatives are possible. Kelman contends that "the creation of a counterform can be a, and the, crucial element in a *kairos* happening" (p. 65). In other words, on Kelman's view, *kairos* points to those moments when alternative states of existence (or, put another way, alternative lifestyles) are both conceivable and achievable.

Hainline (1980) also associates *kairos* with the recognition or perception of different ways of living. For instance, Hainline maintains that both "Jung and Kelman each realized in his own way that we need to apprehend these important moments when unconscious eternal time intersects our conscious linear time, for at these moments, the possibility of illumination, meaning, and wholeness obtain" (p. 330). Although his terminology is somewhat more metaphysical in nature than Kelman's, Hainline's basic conception of *kairos* is otherwise similar. For both authors, *kairos* denotes particular moments when particular individuals can see past the patterns of their current lives and envision new patterns (i.e., Kelman's counterforms). This conception is similar in some ways to the one held by Erikson who, according to Goldwert (1991), considered a kairotic moment to be "a crucial period in which a decisive turn one way or another is unavoidable" (p. 554). The "turn" is decisive as it leads to either progress or regression, integration or retardation (see Erikson, 1963). In other words, individuals must move forward and change their lives or they will remain in the same, potentially destructive, behavioral patterns.

Kelman (1969) indicates that the ability to recognize a kairotic moment, at least within a therapeutic setting, can be learned. He notes that "the therapist's effectiveness with regard to *kairos* requires that he have learned and experienced personally and with patients" (p. 81) a wide variety of psychoanalytic theories and their applications. Kelman also suggests that more novice therapists should observe and work with more experienced individuals. Ultimately, Kelman contends that "with such experience and training such a therapist would earlier and more often sense when the possibilities of a *kairos* would be greater" (p. 81). Thus, the analyst would be forewarned, in a sense, and better able to predict when patients would most benefit from specific treatments. Although Hainline (1980) acknowledges that *kairos* can be recognized, he is pessimistic about our ability to do so. Yet, despite an "always present" *kairos*, we remain "unaware, except for those rare moments of truth when we perceive" (p. 331) our connection to historical time and our own unconscious.

## *Kairos* and the Zone of Proximal Development

In keeping with the previous sections of this chapter, in this section I will examine the role of *kairos* in a domain other than rhetoric. Specifically, I will explore the relationship of *kairos*—as the principle of timing and proportion—and the zone of proximal development, a concept developed by Vygotsky as part of his cultural-historical psychology. However, unlike its explicit incorporation within the three domains discussed above, *kairos* is only an implicit element within Vygotsky's conception of the zone of proximal development (ZPD). Although *kairos* only functions implicitly within the ZPD, nonetheless it is a vital component and, furthermore, provides additional support to my contention that *kairos* is linked to general human performance.

Vygotsky (1934a/trans. 1986) defines the zone of proximal development as the "discrepancy between a child's actual mental age and the level he reaches in solving problems with assistance" (p. 187). In *The Problem of Age*, Vygotsky (1934b/trans. 1998) writes that the "area of immature, but maturing processes makes up the child's zone of proximal development" (p. 202). The ZPD, then, is something of a moving scale which measures, at the low end, the child's "actual mental age" and, at the high end, the "age" typically associated with the child's level of performance with adult assistance. Thus, the eight year old, who can, with assistance, solve problems that a ten year old can solve unaided, has a ZPD of two years. As Wertsch (1991) notes, "Vygotsky examined the implications of the zone of proximal development for the assessment of intelligence and for the organization of instruction" (p. 28).[3] In fact, although contemporary scholarship on the ZPD far exceeds that produced by Vygotsky, the ZPD is an important part of his theories, especially as he integrates it with his conception of internalization and the concomitant development of higher order psychological functions.

As Vygotsky noted repeatedly, there was often a disjunction between school-based instruction and a child's development. Development and instruction, according to Vygotsky (1934a/trans. 1986) "have different 'rhythms.' These two processes are interconnected, but each of them has its own measure" (p. 185). Further, the two measures are rarely synchronized: "the curve of development does not coincide with the curve of school instruction; by and large, instruction precedes development" (p. 185). However, Vygotsky implies that in practice, instruction is often geared towards already developed skills and fails to lead or foster development. Thus, his conception of the zone of proximal development has "practical significance [as a] diagnostic principle" (Vygotsky, 1934b/trans. 1998, p. 203) in that its use can help educators stimulate developing functions through targeted instruction.

In order to be effective, this targeted instruction must be kairotic in nature; that is, the instruction must be timed, such that its implementation coincides with the ongoing development of new psychological functions, and proportioned, such that the level of instruction does not exceed the potential development of the child (as measured by the ZPD). That is, notwithstanding for the rare, prodigal exception, an attempt to teach calculus to a two year old will only frustrate the child and the teacher. Vygotsky (1934b/trans. 1998) makes this point when he states that "teaching that is a little late is also difficult and unproductive for the child, just like that which is a little too early. Obviously, there is also an upper threshold of optimum times for teaching from the point of view of the child's development" (p. 204). Relatedly, Vygotsky (1934a/trans. 1986) writes that "for each subject of instruction, there is a period when its influence is most fruitful because the child is most receptive to it" (p. 189). In other words, there is a "right time" for teaching and learning, a time that would prove more beneficial than its predecessors or successors.

Although Vygotsky generally discusses the ZPD in relationship to a child's problem solving skills, he also points out that the ZPD can be used to ascertain development in other areas. He notes, for instance, that while the diagnostic methodology of the ZPD may be "completely inapplicable" (1934b/trans. 1998, p. 203) for determining potential physical development, the "problem [of measurement] pertains to this aspect of development as it does to all others in completely the same way" (1934b/trans. 1998, p. 203). Physical training will be most effective when it precedes the development of particular physical skills. Our two year old child is as unlikely to learn ballet as he is calculus. In other words, the "timing" and the "proportion" of physical education or training, like the classroom instruction discussed above, determines its potential impact on a child's development.

Vygotsky apparently intended the ZPD, or at least the principles behind it, to be applicable across a number of areas of human development, both psychological and physical. Further, the ZPD helps determine the *kairos*, the appropriate time and level, of instructional events. So conceived, the ZPD serves to link *kairos*—as the principles of timing and proportion—with instruction and development, two activities linked, in turn, to general human performance. Although Vygotsky does not apparently use the term *kairos*, his discussions of the interaction of teaching and development suggest that teaching should be kairotic in nature and, also, that the principles embodied in the *kairos* construct are important to human performance.

These brief reviews of the role of *kairos* in disciplines other than rhetoric do not, in some ways, advance the present study. That is, across three of the areas discussed above—namely, historical studies, theology, and psychoanalysis—the term *kairos* is defined much as it is in rhetoric. With only minor deviations, *kairos* is defined as "right timing" and "due measure" (or "proportion"), a definition similar, if not identical, to that most often adopted by students of rhetoric and writing. Such similarity is not surprising, of course, as most of the scholars were working from a relatively small pool of original sources. Both Kinneavy (1986) and Smith (1986) turn, for instance, to Plato's *Phaedrus* during their investigations into the nature of *kairos*. Notwithstanding the fairly limited amount of source material, the various authors discussed in this chapter often rely on material apparently less well known to scholars in the field of rhetoric. For example, Smith also incorporates references to *kairos* from Plato's *Seventh Letter* and his fourth book of the *Laws*. The various theologians and psychoanalysts discussed above rely even less on the "standard" references, i.e., on those works most frequently cited by rhetoricians in their discussions of *kairos*. Interestingly, with few exceptions, those modern students of rhetoric who have written about various aspects of *kairos* rarely incorporate scholarship from outside their discipline.

Although the definitions of *kairos* typically used by, for example, contemporary students of writing and modern psychoanalysts might differ only slightly, the contexts in which *kairos* is discussed, and the ways in which the construct is employed, vary greatly. As this chapter demonstrates, *kairos* figures prominently in the scholarship of at least some disciplines other than rhetoric. Most importantly, across these other disciplines, *kairos* is linked to human performance. It is occasionally linked, as in the case of the Western Christian theologists, with rhetorical or discursive performance but, more generally, *kairos* is used to explain and understand human performance more broadly construed. Understanding *kairos* more broadly than it is generally conceived within studies of writing and rhetoric is important, I believe, for at least two reasons: First, a broader conception of *kairos* may have significant implications for understanding the nature of shared or distributed cognitive functions, especially as such functions relate to the production and reception of oral and written discourse. Second, *kairos* may figure importantly in such areas as problem-solving, planning, and conflict resolution, especially as each of these is a human "skill" that often rely on the integration of linguistic (e.g., rhetorical) and sensorimotor (i.e., non-rhetorical or physical) aspects of performance for their successful implementation. I will develop these and other points more fully later in this volume.

In some ways, contemporary students of rhetoric are rather late in jumping on the *kairos* bandwagon. *Kairos* has figured in psychoanalysis and historical studies since at least the 1960s; it has been an important part of theology for much of the 20$^{th}$ century. Regardless, the scholarship I have reviewed in this chapter suggests, as I have argued earlier based on other sources, that "*kairos*"—as the principles of timing and proportion—likely governs successful human performance generally and was only later transformed into the rhetorical construct *kairos*. Furthermore, if Vygotsky's views on the relationship between development, learning, and the zone of proximal development are correct, then it seems highly likely that "kairos" emerges developmentally for individuals. The next chapter will explore how these principles of timing and proportion might, in fact, develop for individuals.

## Notes

1. The other two are Plato's *Seventh Letter* and *Phaedrus*.
2. For the sake of readability I am going to refer to the Western Christian theologians whom I am discussing as merely the "theologians."
3. See, also, Valsiner (1988), especially pp. 140-150.

4

# Timing and Proportion in Human Performance

This chapter continues the expansion of the definition and application of *kairos*—as a construct that embodies the principles of timing and proportion in human performance—begun in earlier chapters. This expansion is based, in part, on the etymological work of Onians (1951) and Liddell and Scott (1846) which suggest that the term *kairos* was initially associated with archery and weaving. Further support was found in the extant scholarship of other domains of knowledge. My review of some of this scholarship reveals that *kairos* figures prominently in disciplines other than rhetoric and, most importantly, that *kairos* is applied to the study of non-rhetorical or non-linguistic areas of human performance. Thus, as I have noted previously in this volume, it seems likely that the rhetorical construct *kairos* develops from similar principles that operate in other areas of human performance. Specifically in this chapter I explore several possible explanations for the development of "kairos"—as a construct that embodies the principles of timing and proportion in human performance generally—in individuals. I also begin to point to ways in which "kairos" might be transformed for individuals into *kairos*.[1]

For the individual, the development and transformation of "kairos" into *kairos* may, in part, be explained by appealing to Vygotsky and the psychological tradition of which he is a seminal figure. As I discuss in some detail below, Vygotsky and others suggest that language and problem-solving undergo concomitant development in large part because much problem-solving involves the verbal construction of plans. Furthermore, the construction of plans would seem to constitute an important component of "kairos" in that such plans integrate both temporal and functional aspects of human performance regardless of domain. That is to say that planning is opportunistic. In the discussion of plans and planning that follows I draw on works from the domains of cultural-historical psychology, cognitive psychology, and cognitive science. I also integrate, although somewhat more selectively, scholarship from other fields and disciplines in order to develop certain ideas more thoroughly.

A chief concern for Vygotsky was the development of higher psychological functions and the role that speech (i.e., the "word" for Vygotsky) played in such development. For Vygotsky, one of the most important initial functions of speech is its ability to indicate (generally material objects) and direct attention.

According to Vygotsky, the "development of speech, thought, and all other higher behavior processes proceed" along similar lines. That is, speech is used initially by adults to direct the activities of children. Later, children "participate actively in this indication" function and begin to use it independently of adults (1929/trans. 1981, p. 220). In her article "L. S. Vygotsky's Ideas About The Planning Function of Children's Speech," Levina (1968/trans. 1981) writes that "initially it is through others' speech that the child becomes acquainted with the fact that speech allows us to separate the environment into objects. Then he/she begins to use this same means himself/herself, at first in order to indicate objects for others and then for himself/herself" (p. 285). Thus, speech is initially external to children: speech originates with adults and is used by them to regulate the behavior of children. Subsequently, and as a result of experience with this regulatory function, children begin to use their own speech to regulate their own behavior. With this achievement, however, speech is still external for them. Eventually, with further experience and practice (and perhaps development) children "internalize" (or "interiorize") this external speech, which becomes internal and of course still remains capable of regulating their behavior (see, for example, Luria, trans. 1981, pp. 103-113; Vygotsky, 1929/trans. 1981, pp. 219ff.).

The process of internalization of speech is vital, in Vygotsky's theories, for the development of higher psychological functions because internalized speech provides an instrument which frees the child from only being able to pay attention and respond to immediate perceptual and temporal stimuli ("fields" in Vygotsky's terminology), thereby setting the stage for voluntary performance by the child. The higher psychological functions include voluntary memory, voluntary movement, directed or voluntary attention, and planning and voluntary action. However, even before its internalization, speech is a critical component of planning. Vygotsky notes, for instance, that egocentric speech (i.e., a child's "external" speech) "is an important function of inner speech, in that it plans one's performance" and, in a related vein, a child's egocentric speech contains the "origins of . . . planning" (1926/trans. 1993, p. 165). In a slightly later work, Vygotsky (1930a/trans. 1999) specifically links speech to problem-solving activity, suggesting that speech regulates behavior and fulfills an essential planning function. That is, speech, especially after it has been internalized, can direct voluntary memory and voluntary attention, two key elements in the planning of future courses of action during problem-solving. Relatedly, after speech is fully internalized, behavior becomes less impulsive or reactive and more deliberative.

Gauvain (1999), who uses a cultural-historical framework to investigate the impact of everyday social settings on the planning activities of children, defines planning as "the deliberate organization of a sequence of actions oriented towards achieving a specific goal" (p. 176). Based on her review of numerous studies, Gauvain suggests that children begin to formulate plans around 12 months of age and that children's plans generally increase in complexity as they mature cognitively and socially. Similar findings are presented by Luria (trans. 1981) who writes that "at the beginning of the second year of life (12 to 14 months)" (p. 91) children are capable of planning, although at this age they are not able to moderate their behavior significantly as they have yet to internalize speech. Luria also notes that plan complexity increases with age. Gauvain (1999) argues that there are two central reasons for the growth in planning activity amongst children, both of which enhance the capacity of planning to regulate behavior over longer time periods and more complex kinds of performance:

> First, with development, children are better able to regulate and suspend voluntary action, which permits greater opportunity for mental consideration of alternative procedures prior to action . . . . A second explanation stresses the role of practice in the development of planning. The underlying assumption is that with experience, children come to understand the various components, benefits, and trade-offs of planning and, as a result, show increased incorporation of these skills in their activities. (p. 177)

The first rationale offered by Gauvain is an enhanced version of the Vygotskian theory I discussed briefly above (i.e., planning not only serves to regulate behavior that was previously due to field-dependent involuntary action, it also serves increasingly to regulate voluntary action). Importantly however, Gauvain suggests that children, who develop the ability to "suspend voluntary action," are also developing the capability to wait for the "right moment" to initiate action. Here too, planning can be said to be opportunistic. With respect to the second, Gauvain links children's experience particularly with their social environment, concluding that "research suggests that social interaction is an important context for the development of planning skills" (p. 177). In other words, children become better planners through observation of models, imitation and practice. Notwithstanding its intuitive simplicity, Gauvain's second explanation, and the motivation behind it, are important for reasons I hope to make clear shortly.

Plans and planning activities are kairotic in at least three ways. First, planning involves the sequential arrangement of particular actions. Even in the most basic plans, this sequential arrangement is inherently temporal in nature: For example, step A must be completed before step B; step B before step C; and so on. In more complex plans, the sequential arrangement relies even more on proper timing: For instance, although step B must begin halfway through step A, the two steps must be completed concurrently (e.g., coordinating the arrival of two parties who are coming to a common destination from different distances or by different modes of transportation). As plan complexity increases, so does the importance of the various temporal aspects of individual portions of the plan. Second, the timing of the plan's initiation—and not just of its individual steps—can also be vital. That is, a given plan may succeed or fail, even though the plan's steps were executed flawlessly, if the plan was put into effect too early or too late. Finally, not only are the plan's individual steps sequential, they are also proportional or measured. In other words, each step may require a different level or degree of force for its successful completion. The final stride of the high jumper, while nearly the same length as the first few, is easily the most powerful as he attempts to clear the bar. While exerting the same level of power in the first stride might make the highlight reels, it would otherwise be "unkairotic" and the plan (to clear the bar) would fail.

A person's understanding of "kairos," then, would appear to be a key component of successful planning and plan execution. Further, planning is apparently linked to the acquisition and, in Vygotsky's terms, the internalization of speech; thus, as individual facility with speech increases, so too does the complexity of plans. This link between planning and "speech" is not meant to suggest, however, that an understanding of *kairos* is always situated within rhetorical performance. Although Vygotsky stresses the primacy of speech—a "social" phenomenon—in the development of higher psychological functions, he also acknowledges the role that other sign systems play in this development. For example, in "Tool and Sign in the Development of the Child," Vygotsky (1930a/trans. 1999) writes that:

> A broader study of other forms of symbolic activity of the child shows that not just speech, but all operations connected with the use of signs, with all their differences in concrete forms, display the same patterns of development, construction, and functioning as does speech. (p. 39)

In other words, all "symbolic activity," including the acts of reading and writing which Vygotsky labels "second order" symbolic processes (p. 39), contributes to the development of higher mental functions, such as planning and problem-solving.

Speech and other sign systems fulfill a variety of roles within Vygotsky's theories. Speech is used, for instance, as an aid in problem-solving, to assist in memory recall, and to mediate or regulate behavior. Speech is not, however, synonymous with rhetoric or rhetorical performance. Most importantly, speech, higher psychological functions (e.g., planning), and an understanding of "kairos" are linked to each other and to the social context in which they develop and manifest themselves. Such manifestations occur across and within a number of human performance domains, including but not limited to human rhetorical performance. Although "kairos" is not explicitly discussed by Vygotsky, it seems, nevertheless, that "kairos" or at least a similar notion underlies much of his discussion of human development and human performance. This point is further supported by my discussion of Vygotsky's zone of proximal development (ZPD) in Chapter Three wherein I demonstrated that the ZPD ties together "kairos," education, and child development. Here, too, "kairos" is important in understanding general human performance.

Although Vygotsky clearly places a great deal of importance on the role of sign systems within in his theories of development, he also suggests that practical intelligence precedes speech in the child's development. He notes, for instance, that a great deal of psychological research had been conducted on the premise that "the beginnings of practical intellect may be observed in almost full measure in pre-human and pre-speech periods" in the development of children (1930a/trans. 1999, p. 13). For Vygotsky and other researchers of his era, practical intellect (or practical intelligence) was demonstrated by children through the use of simple tools to solve basic problems (e.g., using a long spoon to push a cookie to the edge of the table in order to obtain the cookie.) Further, Vygotsky believed that children manifested such elementary planning and problem solving skills before they acquired speech.[2] As I noted earlier in this chapter, planning and problem solving are inherently kairotic in nature. If, as Vygotsky contends, planning and problem solving skills develop in children before speech, then it seems reasonable to assert that an understanding of "kairos" (i.e., an understanding of timing and proportion in human performance) develops before an understanding of *kairos* (i.e., an understanding of timing and proportion in rhetorical performance.)

Despite Vygotsky's general agreement with the premise that practical intelligence precedes symbolic activity in children, he asserts that these two lines of development soon merge. It is the transformation of practical intellect by speech (and other sign systems) that leads to the development of higher psychological functions in children. Thus, for Vygotsky, sign systems play a major role in human development. Not surprisingly, they also play a major role in Vygotsky's conception of human phylogeny. He argues, for instance, that speech, and other sign systems, arose only after humans engaged in collective or cooperative labor. This point is also made by A. N. Leont'ev (Leontyev,[3] 1959-a/trans. 1981) who states that "the origin of language can be understood only in relation to the need developing for people in the process of labour to say something to one another" (p. 219).[4] Somewhat more succinctly, Vygotsky (1930b/trans. 1997a) contends that human labor leads to the development of speech which, in turn, leads to the "whole cultural development of the *human mind*" (p. 182; emphasis in the original). Human labor and human language are so interconnected that, according to Vygotsky (1930a/trans. 1999), "the history of work and history of speech can scarcely be understood one without the other" (p. 63). The contentions advanced by Vygotsky and Leont'ev on the role of collective labor in the development of language also suggest that human understanding of "kairos"—which we've seen to be important to the development of planning, problem-solving, and human performance generally—likely predates the human development of language. That is, it seems unlikely that humans could engage in cooperative work activities without at least some rudimentary understanding of "kairos": Flushing the game before the hunters are in place or throwing the spear too soon would, in either case, result in an unsuccessful hunt.

What I have attempted to demonstrate thus far in this chapter is that Vygotsky and others working within the cultural-historical tradition in psychology provide at least one explanation for the development of "kairos"—the principles of timing and proportion in human performance—and its subsequent transformation into *kairos*—the principles of timing and proportion in human rhetorical performance. An understanding of "kairos" apparently develops as children learn planning and problem-solving skills, skills that require temporal and performative sequencing. Further, as these skills are also tied to the acquisition and internalization of symbolic systems (and most especially speech), it seems likely that a child's understanding of "kairos" is also internalized and transformed into an understanding of *kairos*. Yet, and perhaps most importantly, if an understanding of "kairos" (in general performance) is important to collective labor activities, and such activities led to the development of language, it seems clear that "kairos" developmentally precedes *kairos* (in rhetorical performance).

I would now like to turn from cultural-historical psychology to cognitive psychology and cognitive science[5] and thus explore what, if any, explanations for the development of timing and proportion in human performance (i.e., the development of "kairos") might be drawn from the literature of these latter two related fields. The turn from cultural-historical psychology to cognitive psychology might appear a rather sharp one, especially given the ways that some contemporary researchers invoke Vygotsky's name and works. That is, and especially in composition studies, modern scholars often link Vygotsky to social constructionist viewpoints on language and learning, using such links to argue explicitly against cognitive models (see, for example, Bizzell, 1982; Faigley, 1985, 1986; Nystrand, 1986). However, such arguments are based on "narrow" readings of Vygotsky, ones which Cazden (1996) has labeled selective readings of Vygotsky as they serve to support a particular researcher's own perspective. These arguments are "narrow" for at least two significant reasons: First, they rely on, most often, only one or two of Vygotsky's published works; and second, such arguments fail to contextualize Vygotsky's place within the psychological tradition he helped found. A broader readings of Vygotsky, both across his own works and across the works of others, reveals numerous similarities between cultural-historical psychology and cognitive psychology.[6] Although it is beyond the scope of this project to investigate fully these similarities (or, for that matter, the differences that obtain), in what follows some discussion will be focused on them. It is worth pointing out, perhaps, in regards to the matter at hand, that both Mikhail Yaroshevsky, perhaps the leading contemporary Russian/Soviet philosopher of science, and David Joravsky, an American professor specializing in Soviet history, consider Vygotsky a cognitive psychologist. Yaroshevsky (1989) argues, for instance, that Vygotsky initiated the "objective study of the psychology of cognition" (p. 9) while Joravsky (1989) writes that Vygotsky "left prolific disciples, most notably Luria and A. N. Leont'ev, who founded the Vygotsky school of cognitive psychology" (p. 254) and further claims that "Vygotsky is known at home and abroad primarily as a cognitive psychologist" (p. 257).

The importance of planning, as a cognitive function, provides one definitive link between the psychology developed by Vygotsky and his "disciples" and that school of psychology typically labeled *cognitive psychology* in the West. Especially in that latter school, planning is important because, in part, it allows for evaluation, in that the individual can compare the original expectation (of the plan) against the actual outcome (after the plan is implemented). Such evaluation is important for a number of reasons. The first, of course, is that evaluation allows the individual to determine how well the original goal was met and, if necessary, to plan and execute further action in order to better meet the original goal. The second reason is that evaluation allows the individual, once the original goal has been met, to formulate new plans and commence new actions to meet other goals. Evaluation, then, helps to control an individual's actions, at least when such actions are goal-driven. On such a view, the process of evaluation would seem critical to an individual's development of timing and proportion (i.e., "kairos" in a non-rhetorical sense) in that evaluation helps individuals determine the temporal sequencing of their actions.

These two reasons accord well with the discussion advanced by Hayes (1981) on the importance of evaluation as a component of problem-solving. Hayes notes, for example, that "while evaluation is useful in solving simple problems, it is even more useful in solving complex ones" (p. 47). One example given by Hayes of a complex problem is essay writing, as it requires the writer to constantly compare the text under production against the goals and purposes of the original writing task. So defined and delineated, essay writing seems to be a token of a more inclusive type, namely, discursive acts. It seems reasonable to suggest that many, although certainly not all, discursive acts would appear as complex problems and, accordingly, lend themselves to evaluation. At one level, this line of reasoning can be taken as support for the use of the *kairos* construct in the post-hoc evaluation of printlinguistic texts. My previous criticisms of such evaluations were based on the lack of empirical or theoretical data, data which seem necessary to justify the transplantation of the construct *kairos* from its roots in an oral tradition to the modern world of printlinguistic texts. Here then, one can at least theoretically link *kairos* to the post-hoc evaluation of printlinguistic texts provided that two of the criteria used in such evaluation are timeliness and due measure. Such criteria, of course, would only be legitimate evaluation tools if they were bound up within the problem presented by the original writing task (or, more broadly conceived, the original discursive act.)

Of course, as I have discussed earlier in this chapter, both planning and any subsequent evaluation are kairotic in nature in that both activities help individuals sequence their actions across time as well as determine the appropriate levels of force to be applied during the completion of their actions. The activity of evaluation is oriented, at least in part, towards both the past (during the evaluation of past plans and outcomes) and the future (influencing future plans). As Simon (1989) notes, "evaluation functions of some kind are needed to assess the promise of different [possibilities]" (p. 109). In other words, evaluation can occur after a given plan is completed; it can also occur before a given plan is initiated. In such a case, evaluation would be used to compare a plan's likely outcome against the (or $\underline{a}$) desired outcome. If evaluation reveals a significant gap between the two outcomes (i.e., between the likely and desired outcome), then another plan might be developed and evaluated.

The use of evaluation before the initiation of a particular plan is related to the third reason that evaluation is important, namely, that evaluation helps individuals formulate better plans in the future. If plans are evaluated after they are completed, the information provided by such evaluation can be used to shape the development of later plans. Equally important, the evaluation of plans before their initiation helps the individual formulate plans in which the likely outcome (of the plan) more closely matches the desired outcome. In both cases, the results of evaluation can be used at a later date to create better plans. Das, Kar, and Parrila (1996) suggest that planning competency develops both quantitatively and qualitatively, although they also admit that exactly "what develops, however, is still largely an unanswered question" (p. 138). Part of the answer likely lies in a concomitant increase in both planning competency and the number of plans developed and evaluated. In other words, planning competency increases, at least in part, because individuals can use their past planning and evaluating experience to eliminate various alternatives based on their feasibility given the situation at hand. Thus, planning competency (especially when considered in terms of the speed of plan formation) is tied to the individual's knowledge of a particular type of problem: the greater an individual's experience with a given problem type, the faster a plan can be formulated (and the more likely the plan will satisfactorily solve the problem).

The development of planning competency is dependent to some extent then on an individual's preparation (i.e., prior practice.) Such preparation is also important as it leads (or at least can lead) to expertise. As Posner (1988) notes, although "individuals may differ in overall ability or particular abilities" there is an "overwhelming emphasis in the recent cognitive literature on the ability of any person to achieve expert performance with practice" (p. xxxv). Whether such expert performance was demonstrated in chess (see, for example, Chase & Simon, 1973; deGroot, 1966), typewriting (Gentner, 1988; Salthouse, 1984), or in filling dairy orders (Scribner, 1983/rpt. 1997; 1985/rpt. 1997), the individual performers acquired their domain specific expertise through hundreds of hours of practice (if not thousands of hours for the master level chess players.) Once acquired or developed, expertise allows an individual to respond in a timely and proportionate manner "in the moment" of the situation. In other words, expertise enables an individual to better and more quickly perceive the necessity for and the appropriateness of particular actions. Carlson (1997) suggests, in fact, that expertise allows for the "flexible control of action" (p. 258) and that such flexibility "allows for adjustment to temporal constraints, allowing experts to maintain temporal coordination of their activity with demands of the task environment" (p. 258). In other words, experts are more likely to "grasp the concept of propriety of time" (Plato, trans. 1958, pp. 271-272); they are more likely to recognize the "kairotic moment" and then to plan and act accordingly. Again, planning is, at least in part, opportunistic.

Such recognition, of course, and the plans and actions that follow, seem to require that the temporal pacing of the situation in question be such that it allows for reflective planning (e.g., those problem-solving skills discussed earlier) on the part of the individual. In certain situations, however, the temporal pacing can be such that it does not allow for reflective planning; these situations require, instead, a much more immediate response on the part of the individual. One such situation occurs every time a professional baseball player steps into the batter's box. The batter has but a split second to pick up the release of the ball from the pitcher's hand, to identify the rotation of the baseball and determine if it is a fastball, a slider, or a curve (among other possibilities), and to adjust the swing of his bat (which includes the length of his stride, the direction of his stride, the position of his hands, when to begin the swing, etc., etc.) There is little time to "think," and certainly no time to plan. The batter relies on memories stored in both his mind and his body, memories developed over the thousands of times he has swung a bat at a pitch. In short, the batter relies on his own embodied practice, i.e., that performance that relies on the integration of mind and body for its successful completion.

So defined, embodied practice is a concept which unifies the human mind and body rather than distinguishing between the two in conformity with what Ryle (1949) calls the official Cartesian doctrine (p. 11), a doctrine openly questioned by scholars as diverse as Bateson (1972), McNeill (1992), Wilson (1998), and Haas and Witte (2001). Successful embodiment of a particular practice results from, as the term suggests, repetition and preparation and reflects a certain level of expertise in particular performance domains. Unlike practices which occur within performance domains that allow for reflective planning (and evaluation and plan modification), embodied practices generally occur within domains that do not admit such reflexivity. Interestingly, individuals who rely on embodied practices for successful performance in a particular domain often experience some difficulty "explaining" their practices. Rather, such explanations often take the form of time-honored sports clichés: individuals speak of "being in the groove," "locked in," and "being in the zone."

As I noted above, expertise allows individuals to more quickly understand and respond to "the moment" of a given situation. The plans and actions generated by individuals in such situations are generally considered to be largely deliberative or reflective in nature. Embodied practice, however, is a type of expertise by which individuals respond to "the moment" of a given situation through non-deliberative[7] or non-reflective performance. In fact, in those domains where successful performance "relies" on embodied practice, performance is often hindered by various cognitive factors that are external to the practice itself (see, for example, Gentner, 1988). In other words, in certain domains of human performance, and especially in those that involve automatized performance, too much "thinking" can inhibit successful action.

Interestingly, Carlson (1997) notes that there is "some evidence . . . of common timing mechanisms for symbolic and perceptual-motor skills" (p. 268). Such a hypothesized "common mechanism" would, then, govern both the individual's linguistic and physical behavior. It seems likely that if the timing of both linguistic and physical behaviors are controlled by a single mechanism, then during ontogenesis individuals would not develop such "timed" behaviors independently of each other. Rather, it seems more reasonable to suggest that individuals would develop a single principle of timing (in relationship to behavior) and then apply that principle to different areas of their own performance (e.g., discursive acts and physical actions). Such a view accords well with the argument I presented earlier in this chapter, namely that individuals develop the principles of timing and proportion in non-linguistic areas of human performance (i.e., "kairos") prior to the application of these same principles in linguistic (or rhetorical) areas (i.e., *kairos*). Thus, although an understanding of "kairos" (in general human performance) is developed by the individual first, that individual's subsequent understanding of *kairos* (in human rhetorical performance) relies on similar principles and shares a common internal mechanism for its control.[8]

## Notes

1. In an attempt to maintain some typographical distinction between the two, I will refer to the rhetorical construct as *kairos* and the human performance construct as "kairos."

2. Given the point at hand, it is probably worth noting, however, that Vygotsky would have considered it impossible for the child to formulate such plans before the acquisition of language without a concrete situation in hand.

3. I have used what appear to be the most common spellings of names of Soviet-Russian writers (e.g., Vygotsky, Luria, Leont'ev) in that text that I wrote; however, for in-text citations and in direct quotations from primary and secondary sources, I have used the spellings as they appear in the particular publications cited.

4. Both Vygotsky and Leont'ev are drawing, in these discussions, rather heavily on Marx (cite) and Engels (cite).

5. Hereafter I use "cognitive psychology" to refer to both fields except in those cases where I need to distinguish between the two.

6. For a fuller explication of these and related points see Witte, Stephenson, and Bracewell (in progress).

7. "Non-deliberative" in the sense that any such actions are unplanned (except rather globally—the batter "plans" to hit the ball but does not "plan" all of the required supporting actions, relying instead on embodied practice.)

8. It is, unfortunately, beyond the scope of this project to fully investigate just what this common mechanism might be and what factors might be responsible for the transformation of "kairos" into *kairos*.

# 5

# Conceptions of Time, Timing, and Times

This chapter reports on the field research I conducted in support of my project. More specifically, this chapter outlines the following: the particulars of the study itself (including descriptions of the participants, setting, and data collection methods); the methodology used for transcription and data analysis; and descriptions and analyses of the data. (More extended discussions of these analyses and conclusions drawn from such analyses appear in Chapter 6.) Although the direction and scope of the research I report on here was influenced by each of the research questions I identified in Chapter One, my research was most directly influenced by my fifth research question, namely: What, if any, understanding of *kairos* do writers have and how do they employ that understanding when writing?

## The Study

The Subjects/Participants:

The subjects/participants for this research are three journalists who work for the Rebburton Gazette, a major daily newspaper.[1] The Rebburton Gazette is headquartered and published in a mid-sized city (Rebburton) that is part of Anglia, a large Midwestern metro area.[2] A brief biographical sketch of each journalist follows.

Wayne. Wayne is a male who, at the time of the study, had just turned 50, which he indicated was a "hideous age to be." Wayne graduated from high school in the eastern part of the Anglia metro area. He attended a small liberal arts college in the same state, graduating with a degree in English. He has worked at the Rebburton Gazette for 19 years, starting off as a copy editor. Wayne now writes a weekly transportation column which, as he puts it, can be about "anything that has to do with driving." He also writes occasional feature stories and personality profiles.

Marie. Marie is a female in her mid to late 30s who has been at the Rebburton Gazette for three years. Before that she worked for twelve years at a smaller paper located in the northwest section of the Anglia metro area. Maria has a degree in journalism from a state university in the western part of the state. She has a regular "beat" and writes from three to five columns a week on the Rebburton city government. She noted that there is no specific number of columns she is required to write each week but she did add that if she "probably disappeared from the paper for a couple weeks someone might notice." Like Wayne, Marie writes the occasional feature story.

Jimmy. Jimmy is a male in his mid to late 30s who completed both his B.A., with a dual major in English and communications, and his M.A., in creative writing, at a local state university. Jimmy has been at the Rebburton Gazette for nine years; before coming to the Gazette he too worked for a smaller paper in the Anglia metro area, although for only four years. Jimmy is a "local" columnist which, he reports, is rather loosely defined and, while he does write columns which focus specifically on Rebburton, he also writes columns dealing with national events. Jimmy's column appears three times a week. He too writes feature stories periodically.

The three journalists described above have been at the Rebburton Gazette, on average, for just over 10 years. Wayne has been with the paper the longest (19 years), Marie the shortest (3 years). The journalists have, again on average, nearly 16 years of experience writing for newspapers. Here too, Wayne has the most experience (19 years) while Jimmy has the least (13 years).

## Data Sources:

Wayne, Marie, and Jimmy were each interviewed separately; the audio of each interview was recorded for later transcription (see below). Although the interviews took place at the offices of the Rebburton Gazette, they were conducted in a variety of places. Wayne was interviewed in a spare office, Marie in a distant corner of the lunch room, and Jimmy in a small conference room. Despite the differences in locale, each interview was conducted with little or no "outside" interference. That is, the audio recordings were relatively easy to transcribe.

The interviews were fairly unstructured in that no set number or pattern of questions were asked. Rather, the journalists were queried about their education, previous work experience, and current job. Typically, they were then asked about how they chose stories, what factors went into those decisions, etc. More specific follow-on questions were then posed in order to further elucidate what role the dual "principles" of *kairos* (i.e., timing and proportion) played in the journalists' writing practices. Late in each interview, I explained the specific focus of my project and then asked if the journalists had any further thoughts based on that focus.

Although Wayne has the most experience as a journalist, his interview was the shortest, lasting right at 30 minutes. Marie's interview lasted approximately 45 minutes; Jimmy's nearly an hour. In total there was some two hours and fifteen minutes worth of conversation which yielded, after transcription, roughly

58 pages of double-spaced text. These 58 pages of text were the primary source of data discussed below.

The secondary source of data discussed below is an approximately 35 minute long think aloud protocol conducted by Jimmy. After some instruction from the researcher, Jimmy recorded the protocol at his home while working on an upcoming feature story. The protocol was conducted in an environment normally associated by Jimmy with textual production (he almost always wrote at home) during a writing task that was also familiar to him. This protocol yielded some 17 pages of double-spaced text.

## Methodology - Transcription:

The transcriptions of Jimmy's interview and protocol were done by the researcher. The transcriptions of the interviews of Wayne and Marie were done by an outside source. Some twenty minutes of these latter two transcriptions (out of a total of 75 minutes) were spot-checked for accuracy by the researcher. Only two minor discrepancies were found: In one instance the word "speech" was transcribed for the spoken word "piece"; in another the word "use" was transcribed for the spoken word "is." In both cases, the context of the surrounding passages supported the revision of the transcription. The transcriptions done by the researcher were spot-checked by a colleague familiar with the project but otherwise not involved with it. Nearly thirty-five minutes of these two transcriptions (of Jimmy's interview and protocol which totaled some 95 minutes) were assessed for accuracy. The most numerous type of error noted was that of missing words or phrases. In all, there were thirty-three instances noted where words were missing from the transcript. The most common absent word was "that" (7 total instances); each of the following words or phrases were missing two times: kind of, you know, it's, then, and would be. The second most common error found in the transcript is that of a missing "repeated" word. This error occurred a total of fifteen times and occurred when the interviewed subjects uttered a word twice in succession (e.g., "I I" or "the the"). Often either the or second second utterance would be missed on the transcription. The "I I" was missed five times; "the the" three times; and "in in" two times. The third most common error occurred when the reviewer found words in the transcript that were not present on the tape recording. There were seven total instances of this error type; within this error type, the word "and" occurred three times. There were four other errors of various kinds found by the reviewer. Although the number of errors identified by the reviewer appears rather large (especially in comparison to the spot checks of the other two transcriptions), the errors are all rather minor in that they do not affect the semantic content of the transcription. Thus, the transcriptions were taken to be reasonably faithful renditions of the recorded interviews.[3]

Although the data analyzed below was taken from the four transcriptions, the analytic focus was not on the transcriptions themselves but rather on what was said in the transcriptions. That is, given the nature of the research questions guiding this chapter specifically and this volume generally, the conventions of standard transcription (see, for instance, Atkinson and Heritage, 1984, pp. ix-xvi; Potter and Wetherell, 1987, Appendix 1) were not followed as the resulting texts would provide information outside the focus of this project. A similar point is made by Potter and Wetherell (1987) who write that "for many sorts of research questions, the fine details of timing and intonation are not crucial, and indeed they can interfere with the readability of the transcript" (p. 166). Thus, rising and falling intonations, silences between utterances and/or words, verbal "placeholders" (e.g., "uh" and "um"), and various characteristics of pronunciation, among other verbal phenomena often accounted for, are not noted in the transcriptions used for this project.

Additionally, simultaneous and overlapping utterances are generally treated as independent (i.e., non-simultaneous and non-overlapping) utterances; these utterances are inserted in the transcription at that point in the interview when the utterance first started. The remainder of the utterance by the interrupted speaker is then continued after the completion of the simultaneous or overlapping utterance. There is, however, one exception to this treatment. In those instances where the simultaneous or overlapping utterances functioned as *continuers*, the utterances were eliminated from the transcription altogether. Continuers are a specific type of response token that decline "an opportunity to take a full turn [in the conversation], while [displaying] an understanding that the current speaker is producing an extended turn or discourse unit that is not yet complete" (Schegloff, 2001, p. 291. See also Gardner, 2001; Schegloff, 1984; Svennevig, 1999.) Continuers often take the form of "yeah," "uh-huh" or "mm hm"; in the case of this researcher they most often took the form of "okay" or "sure." In those instances where these various utterances served other functions (e.g., as an answer to a question) they were left in the transcription. Again, however, when they functioned as continuers they were not included in the transcription.

## Methodology – Data Analysis:

The analysis of the data was done using a grounded-theory approach (Glaser & Strauss, 1967; Strauss, 1987; Strauss & Corbin, 1994). Such an approach, according to Glaser and Strauss (1967), lends itself to the "discovery of theory from data systematically obtained from social research" (p. 2). That is, coding categories arise from the data; they are not superimposed upon it. This is not to suggest, however, that the data analysis (and indeed the research itself) was entirely inductive in nature. There were, of course, several specific questions guiding the research conducted for both this chapter specifically as well as the volume more generally. Ideally these specific research questions have served as "generative questions" which Strauss (1987) defines as questions that "stimulate the line of investigation in profitable directions" and "lead to hypotheses, useful comparisons, the collection of certain classes of data, [and] even to general lines of attack on potentially important problems" (p. 22). Perhaps the most direct effect of these research questions occurred in the data collection phase of this project although this effect also impacted all subsequent phases of the research. Specifically, the research questions guided the focus of the questions asked during the interviews which, in turn, surely affected the participants' responses. The analysis and discussion of these responses (i.e., the analysis and discussion of the data) was shaped by the nature of the responses themselves. What we see, then, through a linear cause and effect progression, is that the results of this project were impacted by the initial research questions.

Potter and Wetherell (1987) suggest that after the transcriptions are completed the next major step is to "squeeze an unwieldy body of discourse into manageable chunks" (p. 167). However, they provide no clear way to operationalize such a selection process. This point is not lost on Tuffin and Howard (2001) who write that "exactly how the process of coding should be carried out is not made clear" (p. 200) by Potter and Wetherell. Although none of these authors are working from within a grounded theory methodological framework, their concerns are echoed in some ways in much of the literature on grounded theory. Strauss (1987) notes for instance that coding may be "the most difficult operation for inexperienced researchers to understand and to master" (p. 55). There is, however, no indication from Strauss (or indeed others employing grounded theory methodologies) that a "narrowing" of the data set is a necessary or specific step to be undertaken. Rather, Strauss (1987) argues that a solid and early "grounding in . . . data gets researchers away from too literal an immersion in the materials . . . and quickly gets them to thinking in terms of explicit concepts and their relationships" (p. 29). As the questions asked during the interviews were reasonably focused on the subject under investigation, there seemed no sufficient reason to narrow or reduce the data set. Furthermore, the initial coding process served, as Strauss predicted, to keep this researcher from drowning in the pool of data and allowed somewhat more global and/or conceptual relationships to be established and explored.

Following the guidelines laid out by Strauss (1987), an open coding was done of the first transcribed interview (Wayne's). The purpose of this initial coding was to "produce concepts that seem to fit the data" although such concepts are, by definition, "provisional" and subject to extensive revision (Strauss, 1987, p. 28; see also Chapter 3.) The early concepts that were derived from the first analysis of Wayne's transcribed interview were then used during the analysis of Marie's interview. In turn, the concepts that arose from the analysis of both Wayne's and Marie's interviews were applied to the analysis of Jimmy's interview. All the major coding concepts came from the analyses of Wayne's and Marie's interviews; no new concepts were discovered in Jimmy's interview. In other words, a satisfactory level of "theoretical saturation" apparently had been reached. The transcription of Jimmy's think-aloud protocol was used to verify that such a theoretical saturation had been reached, i.e., it was coded to see if any new categories arose in it. Here too, no new categories were discovered. The data set was then limited to the transcriptions of the three interviews; the transcription of the think-aloud protocol was not used in later coding and analytic phases. That theoretical saturation was reached with a fairly limited data set is not as surprising as it may appear on the surface, however, especially given the numerous similarities across the three journalists (e.g., workplace, assignments, experience level, etc.)

Numerous coding passes were done of the three transcriptions which constituted the final data set. During each pass, the coding categories were further refined and/or elaborated as necessary to better accommodate the data. Such successive coding passes are often referred to as "constant comparative analysis" (cf. Glaser & Strauss, 1967; Strauss, 1987; Strauss & Corbin, 1994), such analysis being an essential feature of the grounded theory methodology. The comparisons between the data, the coding categories, and the relationships between the coding categories were continued through the draft and completion of this chapter. This constant analysis helped ensure that the categories adequately represented the data. The early coding passes yielded a two part classification scheme. The first part of the scheme was initially entitled "Conceptions of Time" and comprised of several subparts. (See Figure 1 below.)

Figure 1: Diagram of First Major (Tentative) Coding Category

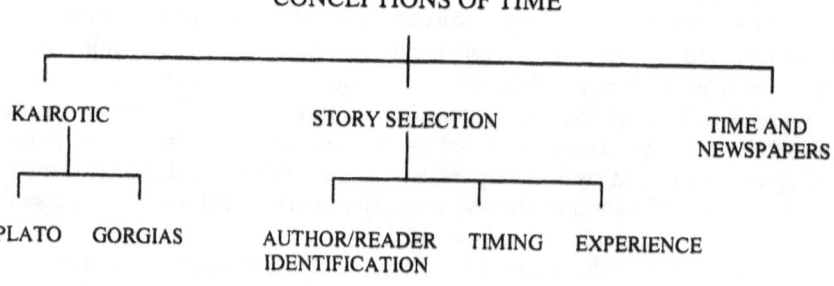

The second part of the scheme was initially entitled "Proportion" and was also comprised of several subparts. (See Figure 2 below.)

Figure 2: Diagram of Second Major (Tentative) Coding Category

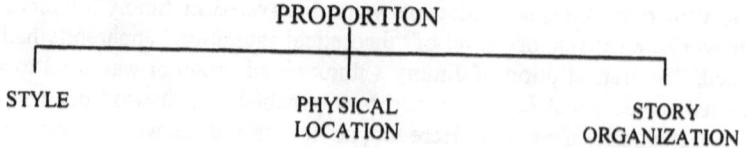

This early conceptualization was eventually replaced by a different two part scheme. The first part of this scheme is entitled "Conceptions of *Kairos*"; the second part "Impacts and Instantiations of Kairotic Conceptions." This model is discussed in further detail below.

The adequacy of the categories (i.e., their ability to properly characterize the date) was also checked by a second coder. Although familiar with the project, the second coder was otherwise not connected with it in any way. Essentially, the outside coder attempted to correlate the assignment of various data segments to the particular coding categories. In other words, the coder used the descriptions of the coding categories to determine if the data segments had been placed in the correct coding category. This "double-check" revealed only a few minor disagreements between the two coders that were easily adjudicated. Relatedly, the independent coder also checked the original transcripts (from which the data was drawn) in an effort to determine if any sections of the transcripts should have been coded but were not. That is, the coder looked for "missed" (i.e., uncoded) data segments. In all, one hundred and twenty (120) data segments from the three transcripts had been coded originally. The outside coder uncovered an additional 10 segments that had not been coded. This suggests that the original coding sequence accounted for some 92% of the available and relevant data.

## Data Analysis – Results and Discussion:

This section details and defines the coding categories that developed from the analysis of the data and provides representative datum for each category. A number of the categories may appear to be somewhat peripheral to the focus of the main research question that guides the research reported in this chapter. They are, nonetheless, included here both for the sake of completeness and for reasons that I hope will become more clear later in this chapter and in Chapter Six. The bulk of the discussion of the importance of the categories and the relationships that obtain between them will be done in the section immediately following this one.

Two major categories arose from the data: The first of these is "Conceptions of *Kairos*." (The second major category covers the impacts of these conceptions and will be discussed later.) The category "Conceptions of Kairos" includes three subcategories, namely, "External Model of *Kairos*," "Internal Model of *Kairos*," and "Proportion" (see Figure 3 below). The last of these three subcategories, "Proportion," is partitioned further into three subdivisions, namely, "Style," "Story Organization," and "Newspaper Organization." Each subcategory and its subdivisions (if any) will be discussed in turn below.

## Figure 3: Diagram of First Major (Final) Coding Category

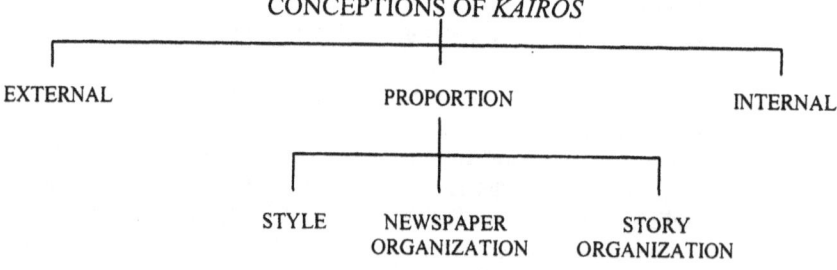

The first major category, "Conceptions of *Kairos*," is something of an umbrella category and is so named as it incorporates, not surprisingly, the three subcategories that are most directly concerned with how the journalists understand "right timing" and "due measure," and how they incorporate those understandings with their production of text. Here, I am using the phrase "production of text" to refer to what is commonly called the "pre-writing" or invention stage as well as those initial "writing" stages (i.e., those stages that occur before major reorganizations or revisions and final editing occur.)

The first subcategory in this group is "External Model of *Kairos*." This subcategory includes data that suggest a view of *kairos* as an independent force or agent that needs only to be recognized by the journalist and, once recognized, acted upon. In other words, on this perspective, *kairos* is external to the writer and the writer's production of text. Here, the writer's production of text can be seen as a response to the kairotic moment. Jimmy, for instance, stated during his interview that "opportunity is out there" and he believes he can "capture [that opportunity]" through the act of writing (J: 511-516).[4] But that opportunity, at least as it relates to a specific event (an event that would be newsworthy), evaporates if not acted upon quickly enough. Marie suggested that there are "timeframes" (M: 185) to ongoing events—timeframes that require a certain expediency in getting the story to press. A similar sentiment was put forth by Wayne when he noted that he often questions whether a story written early in the week will "hold up till the end of the week" (W: 83-84) for publication. In all three of these brief examples, the journalists position *kairos*, especially when defined as "right timing," as an entity located "out there" (i.e., external relative to themselves as writers) and apparently believe they must produce a textual response before the moment disappears.

The second subcategory in this group is "Internal Model of *Kairos*." In contrast to the first major subcategory discussed previously, this subcategory arises from those data which indicate the journalists believe they can write their stories such that the stories are compelling, immediate, and important for their audiences; the journalists can produce their own timeliness. In other words, this subcategory includes data that reveal a view of *kairos* as a force or agent created by the writer; *kairos* is generated "internally" by the writer during the production of text. Marie alluded to this view when she mentioned that after writing a story it "tends to take on a life of its own" (M: 65-66). The ability to create opportunity (i.e., to create a kairotic moment) was linked by Jimmy with *confidence*: the more confident writers are, the more likely they can "make you believe that this is the most important thing you've read" (J: 515). Interestingly, however, and somewhat in contradistinction to Jimmy's previous statements (mentioned immediately above and in the preceding paragraph), Jimmy also claimed that it is "the drudgery of writing every day" that "creates the opportunity" (J: 504-505). These data, then, suggest that the journalists believe they can generate a kairotic moment through their production of text.

The analysis of the data also revealed that the journalists equated an internal model of *kairos* with writing style. In other words, the data indicated that the journalists link the creation of a kairotic moment with their authorial modes. Wayne observed, for instance, that in order for journalists to fully convey their stories, they need to intrigue and challenge their readers (W: 279-282). This same sensibility was echoed by Marie who stated that journalists need to write their stories "the right way" so that readers find the stories "interesting" and "important" (M: 156-157). The importance of style was also evident (as a subdivision) within the subcategory "Proportion." In this case, however, style is not linked necessarily to the creation of kairotic moments; rather, here, style is important because of its impact on the reactions of the readers. In other words, the subdivision "Style" reflects the journalists' concerns with the responses of their readers but not with their concern over imparting (or, more specifically, with creating) the importance of a particular story (such a concern would fall under the subcategory "Internal Models of *Kairos*" discussed above.) For example, Marie stated that word choice was very important (M: 93-95) and something that she agonized over (M: 225-229). According to Marie, she strove to use words that her readers would not find "judgmental" (M: 228-230) especially, as she noted, the Rebburton Gazette enjoyed a "very diverse readership" (M: 230). A similar point was made by Wayne when he admitted, while answering a query about the use of a style guide at the newspaper, that the "nuances [of his writing] can get lost" (W: 170-171) because of the medium and that audience reactions to his stories are often both unexpected and unpredictable (W: 176-178). The importance of style was also alluded to by Jimmy, although perhaps in a more favorable light. Specifically, Jimmy noted that his use of a consistent and predictable style (or "voice" as he put it) allowed him to comment on subjects that had been well covered by various other news media (J: 390-392; 429-436). Although his readers may have come across the story elsewhere, Jimmy reasoned that they had yet to read his take on the subject and, accordingly, they would still find his voice, his style, new and "unique" (J: 391) and, ultimately, worth reading. Jimmy's comments are particularly illuminating as they suggest that writers can create their own particular kairotic moments even if their topic has been well-covered earlier by other writers; the creation of such kairotic moments is, as these data suggest, heavily dependent on the writer's style.

"Story Organization" is the second subdivision within the subcategory "Proportion." This subdivision is based on those data which suggest that the journalists believe that the material organization of a story (i.e., a column or feature printed in the Gazette) affects the response of their readers. During a discussion of some of the differences between newspapers and television, Wayne alluded to this belief when he noted that unlike television journalists he gets the "chance to throw [a story] up on screen and rework it and say, well, if I say this, they're [the readers] gonna think this incorrectly. Let's move this around; let's rewrite this; let's move this up here" (W: 181-183). The importance of a story's organization was also mentioned by Marie. She noted, for instance, that she proofreads her own stories with the two related questions (among others) "Is everything where it should be?" and "Does the organization make sense?" in mind (M: 286-294). The focus on organization is important, according to Marie, because if a story "jumps" (i.e., if it has poor organization) you are likely to lose your readers (M: 294-296). In other words, this coding subdivision reflects the relationship that the journalists conceive between textual structure and their ability to impart a particular story's significance. In the perspective offered by the journalists, well organized texts help readers establish and maintain that text's importance.

The final subdivision in the subcategory "Proportion" is that of "Newspaper Organization." As with the subdivision "Story Organization," this coding category reflects the significance the journalists place on organization, albeit organization at a more global level. More specifically, this subdivision groups together those data dealing with the importance of the overall organization of the newspaper, especially as that organization, like the more molecular organization of particular columns or features within the newspaper, assists readers in determining the import of the individual stories. Wayne indicated, for instance, that they have "major internal discussions" at the Gazette about "how to 'play' stories," that is, about "what page to put them on, what size headlines" to use, and whether or not to include a picture with the story (W: 191-193). The ultimate purpose of these discussions is to figure out "how much attention" (W: 193) to bring to each story especially because, according to Wayne, the physical location of each story in the newspaper serves as "a signal" to the readers; that is, stories on the front page are perceived by readers to be more important than those elsewhere in the paper. A similar point was made by Marie who stated that the impact of stories on readers is partly determined by the location of the stories within the newspaper in part because stories on the front page are more likely to be read (or at least read more thoroughly) (M: 188-198). Jimmy noted that the front page was "prime real estate" and that stories were placed there because they were "important" or, at least, for good reasons (J: 219-221). He also brought up the use of pictures with stories, mentioning that stories which are accompanied by pictures are more likely to be read (J: 232-233).

Those data discussed above reveal the various conceptions of *kairos* held by the journalists interviewed for this study. I would now like to turn to the second major coding category—"Impacts and Instantiations of Kairotic Conceptions"—which addresses the ways in which the journalists' conceptions affect their writing practices. This category is broken down into four subcategories: Story Selection and Timing, Story Selection and Experience, Author/Reader Identification, and Time and Newspapers (see Figure 4 below). Each subcategory will be discussed in turn below. (There were no further subdivisions of these subcategories.)

### Figure 4: Diagram of Second Major (Final) Coding Category

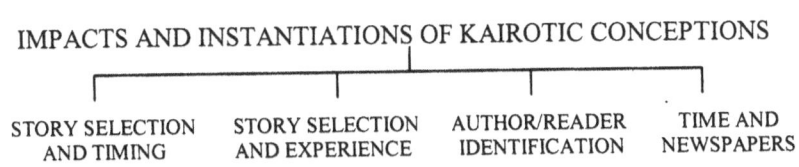

The first subcategory, "Story Selection and Timing," accounts for those data which suggest the journalists determine the "right timing" of a story based on their understanding of the larger (and generally cultural or social) context in which the event (which gave rise to the story idea initially) occurred. For instance, the journalists noted that they are more likely to write about events or people if the subject "has been in the news lately" (W: 67-68) or if the subject is an "ongoing thing" (M: 147). However, the prominence of such events or people is not always generated by the journalists themselves, a fact of which the journalists are very aware. Jimmy stated, for example, that such prominence can be produced through works of literature and film (J: 84-85). Further, both Jimmy and Wayne noted that they often picked stories (or at least the themes or topics for stories) based on the stories' connections to either annual events (e.g., holidays, anniversaries) (W: 92-93; J: 288-294) or to "universal" (and often recurring) events (e.g., the death of a pet, a child's first day of school) (J: 266-275).

"Story Selection and Experience" is the second subcategory grouped under the major coding category "Impacts and Instantiations of Kairotic Conceptions." Grouped within this subcategory are those data which reveal the reliance of the journalists on their on-the-job experience when selecting topics for the columns.[5] When asked what criteria she used to select stories, Marie claimed that it was "ninety percent gut instinct from being in the business" (M: 52) and "largely based on experience" (M: 71). In a lengthy discussion about the impact of experience on his writing practices, Jimmy noted that his growing experience had led him to be a more consistent writer, not only in terms of his style or voice but also in terms of his story selection. He often wrote about the "predictable subjects" (J: 358) as his experience had taught him that he no longer needed to be "totally different [or] totally unique" (J: 359); rather, he now considered himself in a "conversation" (J: 394) with his readers whom, he believed, wanted to hear his take on events. Taken together, these comments suggest that, at least in part, the journalists' ability to determine the "right timing" for particular subjects developed concomitant with their expertise (as journalists).

The third subcategory, "Author/Reader Identification," incorporates data which indicate that the journalists determine the "right timing" or "proportion" of a story based on a commonality they perceive that they (as writers) share with their reading audience. Jimmy alluded to such a perceived identification when he stated that his job "requires being sensitive to the moment of how people . . . are feeling about something," a sensitivity that he likens to being a "mirror for how people are thinking" (J: 381-383). As a columnist, he considers himself at his "best" when he's "being the guy who's saying 'here's how I think we're feeling about this and I'm one of you, I'm one of the people who's feeling that way'" (J: 384-386). Although Wayne claims that he doesn't "sit there and try to think of who's out there reading" his columns (W: 282-283), he does note that he often chooses stories on the "ridiculously basic" premise that "if it seems interesting to [him], [he figures] it's gonna be interesting to a lot of other people" (W: 38-39). This subcategory reflects, in some ways, the journalists' apparent belief that they and their audience share a mutual recognition of a particular kairotic moment.

"Timing and Newspapers" is the fourth and final subcategory within this second major category. This data grouping focuses on the journalists' perceptions that "timing" and/or "proportion" are inherent aspects of the newspaper business. Marie addressed this perception directly when she noted that "timing" and "timeliness" were "built into the business" (M: 321-322). She noted, however, that major papers will often let the smaller papers "win the little war" on the "new nugget" (i.e., the new story), but that the larger papers will "blow [the smaller papers] away on the weekend with the big story that's written by a better writer than [the smaller papers] probably have on [their] staff, that's got more research" and more time to be written (M: 387-391). Wayne also discussed this perception when he noted that "we're in the communication business so if something is significant . . . we'd better get it out there or we're not doing our jobs" (W: 118-120). This point was also made by Jimmy who noted that "if there was a chart, wherever the highest point in terms of importance is [that is] also going to be the highest point in terms of how much time you have to say something about it" (J: 158-160). In other words, journalists need to comment on important events before the kairotic moment disappears. Interestingly, the interview segments included here as data reflect both the internal model of *kairos* and the external model of *kairos* (discussed above) held by the journalists. That is, Marie's remarks rely on an internal model: the major newspapers (as represented by their journalists) will create a new kairotic moment for a particular story, even though that story has already been covered by other, smaller newspapers. The observations of Wayne and Jimmy suggest that the kairotic moment is created by forces other than the journalists themselves which is in keeping with an external model of *kairos*.

This concludes the more low-level discussions of representative data and their analyses. Chapter 6 will continue these discussions, building off the preliminary analyses of the data offered here. Various conclusions drawn from these analyses will also appear in the following chapter.

## Notes

1. All names (including those of the newspaper, the participants, the towns, etc.) are pseudonyms.

2. The city has a population just over 200,000 while the metro area includes some 3,000,000 people.

3. It should be noted that the transcription assessment done by the outside reviewer was not re-checked for accuracy and discrepancies. As none of the errors noted by the reviewer affected the semantic content of the transcriptions, I did not feel such a "double-check" was necessary.

4. Citations of primary data are noted by the first letter of the journalists' pseudonyms and the line number(s) from the corresponding interview transcription. Although the transcriptions themselves are not included, I have left the citations in place to better clarify which journalist is being quoted. I would also offer that the citations serve to bolster my argument that the various conceptions of *kairos* identified in the text proper are indeed held by all the journalists.

5. Although closely related to the first subcategory, "Story Selection and Timing," discussed above, the subcategory "Story Selection and Experience" is distinct as it points to the possible development of an understanding of *kairos* (as a rhetorical construct), as opposed to the more fully evolved understanding and subsequent application of *kairos* implied in the previous subcategory. This subcategory also serves as something of a link between the subcategory "Story Selection and Timing" and the subcategory "Author/Reader Identification." These two points will be further elaborated in Chapter Six.

# 6

# Writing Time and Timing Writing

This chapter continues the analysis and discussion of those data first reported on in Chapter 5. As noted previously, the analyses contained in Chapter 5 were of a rather low-level and/or preliminary nature. Those analyses offered here are intended to be both more global and definitive in nature. Further, this chapter develops a number of conclusions based on the analyses from both the previous chapter as well as the current one and, perhaps most importantly, begins to incorporate material from the first four chapters of this volume into the present discussion.

## *Kairos*: Conceptions, Conflicts and Creation

"Conceptions of *Kairos*" was one of two major conceptual categories that arose from the analysis of the data (see Chapter 5). This major category was further broken down into three subcategories: "External Model of *Kairos*;" "Internal Model of *Kairos*;" and "Proportion." For the purposes of the present section I would like to concentrate on the first two of these three subcategories, namely, the "External Model" and the "Internal Model." (I will return to the subcategory "Proportion" later in this chapter.) Again, briefly, the "External Model of *Kairos*" incorporates those data that suggest a view of *kairos* as an independent force or agent that must be recognized and acted upon (by the journalists); the "Internal Model of *Kairos*" incorporates those data which suggest a view of *kairos* as a force or agent created by the journalist. What is perhaps most interesting about these two coding subcategories is that they emerged at all from the grounded analysis. That is, despite the somewhat antithetical definitions of the subcategories, all three journalists interviewed for this study seem to hold and employ both models of *kairos*. The data suggest that the journalists probably believe that the "right timing" can be both external or independent of them (and their writing practices) and internal or dependent on them (and their writing practices).

This seemingly contradictory finding is further complicated by certain data that suggest that the journalists' conception of the external model of *kairos* is itself dualistic in nature. That is, as previously discussed in Chapter 5 and immediately above, the journalists revealed a view of "right timing" as an independent force or agent. Such a view, of course, accords well with Plato's notion of the "propriety of time," which he posits as an external (i.e., independent) force which need only be recognized by the rhetor and acted upon. Plato (trans. 1995) writes in the *Phaedrus* that students of rhetoric could call themselves rhetoricians only after they had acquired a "knowledge of the times for speaking and for keeping silence" (p. 553), a passage which implies that the "time for speaking" is temporally limited or finite in duration. However, certain data (within the coding subcategory "External Model of *Kairos*") suggest that the journalists maintain a conception of "right timing" that is perhaps even more "ideal" than Plato's original conception. Marie, for instance, noted that "features have a pretty good shelf life" (M: 169); they are often, in her words, "evergreen" (M: 169), a term she defined with the single word "timeless" (M: 177). While discussing a current feature article she had completed recently, Marie admitted that it could have been published six months later with little effect on the immediacy or importance of the story (M: 159-160). The same point was made by Jimmy who stated that a column he had written lately "could have been done five years ago [or] five years from now and it wouldn't have been different" (J: 60-61). Such perspectives on "right timing" are essentially Platonic in so much as they posit *kairos* as a force or agent independent of the rhetor. They are also, however, fundamentally different in that such perspectives do not temporally demarcate or limit *kairos*. At least for the journalists, the timing for the publication of features on certain subjects is apparently always "right" or "opportune." Thus, as I noted previously, not only do various data suggest that the journalists maintain both an external and an internal model of *kairos*, the data also point to a bifurcated external conception, with one part that is temporally limited (what I am referring to as the "standard" external model) and one part that is temporally unlimited (what I am referring to as the "durable" external model).

The data reveal clearly that the journalists (as writers and/or rhetors) do not see themselves as playing a part in either the creation of the "temporally limited" external *kairos* (i.e., the more "standard" conception) or its "temporally unlimited" counterpart (i.e., the "durable" conception). Rather, for the journalists, the "right timing" credited to either of the two external models is created by or because of the actions of forces or agents that are separate and distinct from the journalist. These forces or agents may be best described as *actants*, a term borrowed from actor network theory (see, for example, Latour, 1987; Pickering, 1992). According to Myers (1996), "researchers in actor network theory use the semiotic term *actant* rather than *actor* as part of an attempt to find a vocabulary that does not presuppose the kinds of actors the researcher will find" (p. 11; emphasis in the original). In other words, actants may be human or not. Myers insightfully demonstrates that even cracks in a nuclear reactor are actants as those cracks "become complex mixtures of the social and the natural, defined by scheduled measurements of growth rate, over time, within parameters, with various possible causes" (p. 30). Perhaps most importantly, the cracks set in motion an intricate pattern of actions, actions carried out by other actants who formed part of the relevant network. Before any such actions are completed, however, the particular actants involved must first recognize the situation's exigency, an exigency created in Myers' example by the very real (although only possible) danger presented by a leaking nuclear reactor.

Myers notes that "actor network theory is not so much a theory as a set of methodological principles about what actors are relevant and how they are constructed" (p. 10). These principles can be seen in the work of Star (1991, 1995) and others who have explored how actants become linked with other actants and how such actants use these resultant networks to establish and exercise power. One common theme that emerges from these studies is that non-human actants can exert very real and very direct pressures on human actants, creating an exigence which those humans come to recognize and act upon. In fact, as Croissant and Restivo (1995) point out, "the relative stability of social boundaries and networks over a long period of time gives rise to systems for which we can determine degrees of autonomy" (p. 53). In other words, certain actants as well as the networks to which they belong are very durable and their very durability imbues them with agency. More to the point for my purposes here, both human and non-human actants seem able to create kairotic moments or, at least, to create the conditions necessary for (other) human actants to create such moments. All three of the journalists commented that if a particular subject has been receiving a great deal of publicity recently, the time may be right for a newspaper story on that subject. The subjects mentioned by the journalists were both human and non-human: a particular individual, an annual event, an article published in another newspaper. In the terminology of actor network theory, these subjects are actants, actants which help give rise to kairotic moments that are then recognized and responded to by the journalists.

Nonetheless, the link proposed here between the study of writing and rhetoric and actor network theory generally and between *kairos* and actants specifically is, at this stage, a fairly tenuous one. It may also be a link that, as Myers (1996) puts it, might "antagonize all well-trained researchers in rhetoric" (p. 11). Myers continues:

> Classical rhetoric recognizes humans as the only actors—all other entities are resources to be brought into arguments. Classical rhetoric clearly demarcates the natural and the social, and devotes its attentions to the latter. Classical rhetoric deals with the associations of humans—speaker and audience. Writing researchers have perhaps become used to postmodern challenges to the rhetorical subject . . . . Actor network theory is in a way even more disorienting, because it asks us to imagine a rhetorical situation in which everything is a possible actor, including the piece of paper. (p. 11)

And, as Myers ably demonstrates, not only "pieces of paper" but "cracks in nuclear reactors" can, in certain contexts, seemingly exert real pressures on real people to complete real actions. As I've noted above and will continue to expand on in what follows, the journalists I interviewed reported that various actants, be they individuals, annual events, or previously published texts, influenced various aspects of their writing practices, including their understanding of a story's timing and proportion. Ultimately then, the term *actant* seems to hold some explanatory potential for adequately describing how various entities or agents contribute to the creation of kairotic moments, especially as such moments are reflected in at least two of the models of *kairos* (namely, the standard and the durable external models) that the journalists apparently routinely employ as part of their writing practices.

Since any newly created kairotic moments are temporally limited, the actions of the journalists must be completed within a finite, if difficult to define, span of time. Occasionally, journalists will write columns some time in advance of when the column will be actually printed. Although such a practice can alleviate the pressures of a deadline, it brings with it a different set of concerns. One such concern was addressed specifically by Wayne who commented that a personality profile he had completed on one local celebrity had the words "Alive and Well" in the story's proposed headline. However, by the time the profile made it to print, the subject had suffered a major heart attack and nearly died (W: 135-140). (Needless to say, the headline was changed.) Perhaps more to the point, Marie noted that when she sees a newsworthy event she also knows that "there's probably a timeframe to it" (M: 185) and, accordingly, she needs to get the story into print before that timeframe disappears. An understanding of "timeframes" and timing is apparently vital to the journalists because, as Jimmy stated, even if the column is "the greatest thing" he's "ever written but . . . it's a week late, it's not going to have the resonance that it would have [had]" (J: 524-525) had it been published earlier (and temporally "nearer" the event that sparked the column).

As noted above, the external model of *kairos* (in either of its two forms but most specifically in its "standard" form) identified through analysis of the data is created by actants—by pieces of paper and cracks in reactors—that are independent or external to the journalists. Although the internal model of *kairos* is also created by actants, those actants are always human. They are, in the terminology of actor network theory, actors. And, perhaps most germane here, those actors are always the journalists (as writers or rhetors) themselves. That is, the journalists believe they can create "right timing" through their production of written texts. Interestingly, the creation of a kairotic moment is invariably linked by the journalists with style. Jimmy noted, for example, that "confident" writers can create opportunity; they can "make you believe that this is the most important thing you've read" (J: 514-516). Both Wayne and Marie claimed that they needed to intrigue, challenge and interest their readers in order to get their points across (W: 279-282; M: 156-157). In each case, the journalist relied on style (e.g., voice, tone, word choice) to capture and maintain the interest of their readers; they each used various stylistic devices to enhance and, perhaps most importantly, to impress upon their readers the importance and immediacy of their topic.

Although there are fairly identifiable actants at work in the creation of both the standard external and the internal models of *kairos*, those actants responsible for the creation of the durable external model are less easily named. Certainly, this latter conception (i.e., the conception of *kairos* that it reflects) occurs because of the actions (and possibly inactions) of both human and non-human actants. What is less certain, however, is how the actions of such actants can sustain a kairotic moment over prolonged periods of time. These timeframes may, apparently, last from three weeks (the longest period mentioned by Wayne [W: 130]) to six months (mentioned by Marie [M: 159-160]) to five years (mentioned by Jimmy [J: 60-61]). Interestingly, there appears to be no definitive correlation between the subject matter (i.e., topic) and the creation of a durable Platonic *kairos*. The topics that correspond to the time frames noted just above ranged from the clichéd "local boy made good" (Wayne's subject) to an ongoing legislative process (Marie's subject) to stories about World War II (Jimmy's subject). In each instance, however, the journalists perceived that the relevant actants had (perhaps unwittingly or at least without volition) created a very durable kairotic moment. Not only did the journalists recognize these moments, they also recognized that such moments did not require an immediate response (i.e., such moments were, practically speaking, not bound by time or timing).[1]

## *Kairos*: Creation and Development

The standard external model of *kairos* (and its durable derivative) requires the agency of actants that are outside to and independent of the rhetor. It is, then, somewhat less "rhetorical" in nature than the internal model which relies on the agency of the rhetor for its creation. In other words, the external model can be created through non-discursive or non-rhetorical performance (the resulting kairotic moment need only be recognized by the rhetor); however, the internal model can be created only through discursive or rhetorical performance. The reliance on external actants suggests that the standard external model provides something of a bridge between the "kairos" construct of general human performance (identified and discussed in Chapter 4) and the *kairos* construct of human rhetorical performance. Plato's (trans. 1995) most direct discussion of *kairos* notes that a rhetor must be able to recognize "the times for speaking and the times for keeping silence" (p. 553). In other words, the rhetor must be able to identify a particular kairotic moment which results from the interaction of any number of external actants, actants which remain unspecified by Plato or, for that matter, any of the classical Greek or contemporary rhetorical scholars who treat the *kairos* construct. This ability (i.e., the identification of the proper moment for rhetorical action) is similar to the ability that must surely have been necessary for the archer or the weaver, as actors performing within the two domains of human performance etymologically associated with *kairos*, to successfully complete their actions. Both the archer and the weaver need to "read" the external conditions correctly to either hit the target with the arrow or pass the woof through the threads, respectively. (See the previous discussions of Onians (1951) and Liddell and Scott (1846) in Chapters 1 and 2.)

Both the standard and the durable external models of *kairos* require the rhetor to assess and evaluate various factors before initiating discursive activities. These factors are, however, part of the environment in which the rhetor is operating. They are not, in other words, brought into a given context by the rhetor, nor are they created by the rhetor specifically for that context. On such a view, *kairos* functions as a tool—a tool that is used but not made by the rhetor.[2] The internal model of *kairos* also functions as a tool for the production of discourse but, in contrast to the external models, it also requires the rhetor to "make" as well as use it. According to Vygotsky (1930b/trans. 1997a), the production of tools, as opposed to the use of materials gathered from the material environment as tools (e.g., the use of a stick as a fishing pole), is a key difference between humans and other animals, especially as regards their respective cognitive developments (pp. 178-179). This is not to suggest, of course, that the ability to recognize and subsequently use an external model of *kairos*, a tool that is external to the rhetor, is an ability possessed by other (non-human) animals. Rather, it is meant to suggest, at the least, that the two external models of *kairos*, which require only the use of a tool, likely precede developmentally their internal counterpart, which requires the production *and* use of a tool.

The external models of *kairos* are likely developed by individuals prior to the internal model for at least one other important reason. As discussed above, the external models rely on external actants which create kairotic moments; in turn, the rhetor must recognize these moments and act accordingly. Such an ability (to recognize the moment) is a perceptual function; it is, paraphrasing Vygotsky (1930a/trans. 1999), an "integral" function in that it links perception to external action. The internal model, on the other hand, is more "analytic" in nature; it relies not on a link between perception and external action but on a link between cognitive processes and external action. Although in both cases, the end result is the same (i.e., "external action" or, more specifically, the production of discourse), the initial stimulus originates in different places: The stimulus is external for the external models and internal for the internal model. Again, this is not meant to imply that using an understanding of *kairos* based on an external model for the production of discourse does not involve cognitive processes. Such is certainly not the case. The external models require the rhetor to produce discourse in response to a kairotic moment created by various external actants. Although textual production is an end result in such a conception, such production is not a factor in the creation of the kairotic moment itself. The internal model, on the other hand, requires the rhetor to produce discourse to create the moment. Within the internal model, discourse is both stimulus and response. Within the external model, discourse is only a response: a response to current conditions created by external actants. It is more similar then to the archer who must gauge, among other factors, the wind's direction and speed and the target's distance and speed in order to respond properly (i.e., hit the target with the arrow). The archer is responding to these actants; he does not create them. This analogy suggests, as noted earlier in this chapter, that the *kairos* of the external models bridges the span between the original etymological associations of *kai-*

*ros* and the more "rhetorical" *kairos* of the internal model. Moreover, if an understanding of "kairos" within general human performance develops in individuals before an understanding of *kairos* within rhetorical performance (see Chapter 4) and if a external model links the original meanings of *kairos* with the internal model, it seems reasonable to suggest that an understanding of an external model of *kairos* develops in individuals before an understanding of an internal model of *kairos*. Finally, it underscores the point that an understanding of "right timing" can be an important tool for problem solving both within general human performance and within rhetorical performance.

## *Kairos*: Production and Evaluation

As I first noted in Chapter 1 and discussed more thoroughly in Chapter 2, contemporary scholars of writing and rhetoric have used the *kairos* construct as a post-hoc tool for the evaluation of written discourse. Further, they have done so without adequately justifying either theoretically or empirically their transformation of *kairos* from its origins as a tool for the production of oral discourse into a tool for the evaluation of written discourse.[3] One goal of this project is to provide, if possible, either the theoretical or empirical data necessary to support just such a transformation. Unfortunately, such support could not be found in the transcribed interviews and think-aloud protocol. In fact, very little of the data gathered from the journalists could be seen as reasonably supporting the transformation of *kairos* found in recent investigations into writing and rhetoric. There are, nonetheless, two clusters of data that might be considered as support for this modification of the *kairos* construct.

The first cluster of data is drawn from my interview with Marie. I asked Marie if she ever looked back and realized that she should have written about a particular event sooner. She answered that she had and attributed such a realization to a particular event's "outcome" or its progression (i.e., its growth in terms of newsworthiness) (M: 58-62). She tempered this answer somewhat, however, when she noted that stories often take on a "life of their own" due to the fact that they were written (generally by her) and had subsequently appeared in a major daily paper (M: 65-66). Such statements imply that Marie does in fact use her understanding of "right timing" to evaluate whether or not the production of particular written texts would have been appropriate at a given (temporal) point in the past. Of note here is that her evaluation does not extend to judging the appropriateness of written texts produced in the past; rather her evaluation is focused on whether or not such texts (which do not, in fact, exist and are therefore hypothetical in nature) should have been produced at all. Further, her evaluation is always focused on whether she should or should not have produced (these hypothetical) texts; it is not concerned with judging the relative merits of texts produced by other authors. Thus, even such a "backward" glance through time is more concerned with various aspects of the production, rather than of the evaluation, of printlinguistic texts.

Interestingly, this "evaluatory" focus is based initially on a conception of *kairos* decidedly more internal in nature than external. Marie's statements revealed a certain level of ambivalence about her ability to evaluate the "right timing" of a newspaper column which had been written in the past. Apparently it was difficult for Marie to pinpoint the "exact" *kairos* for a story she had written because, as she noted, the production and publication of a story in the newspaper gave the story a "life of its own" (M: 66). In other words, her text created or instantiated a kairotic moment for the particular subject matter at hand. Nonetheless, after the initial publication of her column, the story's "life" was apparently out of her hands. Marie noted that particular issues addressed in a given story were "rarely . . . resolved" (M: 63-64) quickly and continued to be newsworthy for some time. Seemingly, then, Marie's creation of an internally-based kairotic moment (at least conceptually or definitionally) became, at least in part, an actant that contributed in turn to the creation or sustainment of an externally-based kairotic moment. Marie's production of text becomes its own self-fulfilling prophecy or, more darkly, its own vicious circle: Writing the story may serve to justify and/or determine (i.e., require) more writing about the story. In other words, the created kairotic moment may not be so easily abolished.

The second cluster of data that might also be considered support for the transformation of the *kairos* construct from production tool to evaluation tool can be found in the subcategory "Author-Reader Identification," a subcategory contained within the major coding category "Impacts and Instantiations of Kairotic Conceptions." In Chapter 5 I suggested that the subcategory "Author-Reader Identification" accounts for those data which suggest the journalists determine the "right timing" or "proportion" of a story based on a commonality they perceive that they (as writers) share with their reading audience. In other words, the journalists attempt to judge the merits of a story from the perspective of their readers. Jimmy's "hypothetical" readers are, in fact, rather concrete; his readers are his parents and he evaluates potential columns by asking himself what his "parents [are] going to feel like reading over their coffee" in the morning (J: 322-323). Wayne's reader is also concrete as he typically casts himself as both the writer and reader. Wayne claims that he doesn't worry about the audience evaluation as he doesn't typically "think of . . . who's out there reading" his story (W: 282-283). Rather he evaluates the piece himself, placing himself in the role of reader and evaluator and asking himself if he would "read this thing?" (W: 283).

One difference here is that both Jimmy's readers and text are abstract entities, at least in so much as his readers (which do exist—although elsewhere) never actually read the text in question (which only exists in Jimmy's mind). On the other hand, Wayne's reader (i.e., himself) exists and reads/evaluates the text in question, which exists in printed form. Despite these differences, both journalists rely on a conception of *kairos* as a tool for production, not a tool for evaluation. This is clearly the case for Jimmy who, although evaluating the "right timing" or "proportion" of a story, is doing so before the story has been produced, i.e., before the story has been written down, edited, and published in the newspaper. Jimmy's assessment occurs during the production of discourse; the moment's *kairos* is evaluated within the context of production. Wayne's assessment may also be said to occur within the context of production in as much as his evaluation of his draft is done before the text is published. In other words, like Jimmy, Wayne gauges his text against the kairotic moment before the text becomes "discourse"; his evaluation is done in order to guide the further and, most importantly, the immediate production of printlinguistic text. Interestingly, like the case of Marie discussed earlier in this section, Jimmy and Wayne only evaluate their own texts; they do not employ their understandings of *kairos* for the post-hoc evaluation of texts written by others.

Ultimately, then, it seems reasonable to suggest that these two clusters of data do not, in fact, support the transformation of the *kairos* construct by contemporary students of writing and rhetoric from a tool for the production of oral discourse into a tool for the evaluation of written discourse. This is not to imply, however, that this transformation lacks *any* foundation, merely that this research did not provide it. (This topic will be further addressed in Chapter 7.) Nonetheless, the analysis of these two clusters of data does reveal that the journalists operate with a conception of *kairos* fairly similar to that advanced by Aristotle and, to a lesser degree, Isocrates. More specifically, both Aristotle and Isocrates implied that *kairos* could be employed as tool at the beginning as well as the end of textual production. In other words, the *kairos* construct helps to initiate as well as conclude discursive output; the construct provides a set of standards (i.e., "right timing" and "proportion") by which evaluation can be undertaken during production.

## *Kairos* as Proportion: Style, Organization, and Visuals

This section continues the exploration of the three conceptions of "right timing" identified previously that the journalists appear to work with during their selection of topics and production of text—the standard external model, the durable external model, and the internal model—while extending the exploration into the second common definition of *kairos* as "proportion." As I noted earlier, both of the external models were created by actants external to the journalists while the internal model was created by the journalists themselves largely through the use of various stylistic or rhetorical devices. This is not to imply, however, that "style" is not important to at least the standard, if not also the durable, external model of *kairos*. As we can discern in Plato's (trans. 1995) discussion of *kairos* in *Phaedrus*, not only must the rhetor be sufficiently knowledgeable in order to recognize a particular kairotic moment (the "knowledge of the times for speaking and for keeping silence [p. 553]), but the rhetor also must be able to "make a practical application of a certain kind of speech in a certain way to persuade his hearer to a certain action or belief . . . [and must distinguish] the favourable occasions for brief speech or pitiful speech or intensity" (p. 553). In other words, even after recognizing the "propriety of time," the rhetor needs to be able to properly use any number of stylistic or rhetorical devices in order to properly persuade the audience. Like the internal model identified earlier, the external model of *kairos* also relies in part on style. In other words, although the rhetor may be able to fully recognize a kairotic moment, the rhetor's audience may not and, as a result, the rhetor must employ various stylistic features to convince the audience that not only is the rhetor's discourse important but that now is the appropriate time for its production. The connection, or interweaving, of style with the standard external conception of *kairos* may help explain, at least in part, Aristotle's somewhat ambivalent treatment of the *kairos* construct. As I demonstrated in Chapter 2, Aristotle's more abstract discussions of *kairos* most closely follow Plato's definition of the construct. however, in those passages where he discusses *kairos* in relationship to his own production of text, his treatment of the construct more closely follows a Gorgian model. Plato's conception of *kairos* exhibits, of course, some similarities with the external model of the construct I have proposed: chief among these, both constructs position *kairos* as a force or agent external to the rhetor/writer. Likewise, the internal model of *kairos* I have advanced in this volume displays some affinities with Gorgias' views of the construct: most importantly here, both constructs position kairos as a force or agent created by the rhetor/writer. Ultimately then, on the one hand, Aristotle's theory posits *kairos* as a force or actant independent of the rhetor; on the other hand, however, Aristotle's practice posits *kairos* as a force or actant that is dependent on the actions of the rhetor.

Although style figures importantly in both the internal and external models of *kairos*, it is also important as an element of "Proportion" which is both a principal definition (or, perhaps more succinctly, a principal translation) of *kairos* as well as a major coding category derived from the data gathered for this project. As a subcategory of "Proportion," style is not necessarily linked to the creation of a kairotic moment. It is nonetheless a "kairotic" feature in that it helps the journalists impart or enhance the importance of a particular story: the journalists use style to convey "due measure" to their readers. As discussed in Chapter 5, the journalists appeared keenly aware of the impact that their use of various stylistic and rhetorical features could have on their audience. Such features include word choice (both in terms of a word's complexity and its potential to be considered overly harsh or judgmental), syntactical elements (especially in terms of sentence complexity), voice/tone, and textual structure.

The journalists' concern with the structure of a text also manifested itself in the subdivisions "Story Organization," the second of three such subdivisions grouped under the subcategory "Proportion" (which is, in turn, grouped under the major coding category "Conceptions of *Kairos*.") Some of the data collected within this subcategory suggests that the journalists maintain that the structure of a story impacts how their readers perceive the story. As Wayne noted, he has the opportunity to rewrite a column, to change its organization, so that his readers don't misread his text and come away with a misleading or inaccurate assessment of the story or its importance (W: 181-183). Wayne (W: 303-308) and Marie (M: 217-219) both alluded to important differences between the organization of "hard news" pieces and features (e.g., personality profiles), differences that allow the reader to assess quickly the significance or value of a particular story. The journalists apparently believe that a story's organization helps create a sense of importance, a sense of "proportion" or "due measure," for their readers.

Perhaps not surprisingly, the journalists also believe that the newspaper's organization helps readers differentiate or rank order the importance of the various columns printed in the newspaper. This belief is reflected in the data grouped under the subdivision "Newspaper Organization" within the coding subcategory "Proportion." Wayne claimed that the newspaper staff has "major internal discussions about how to play stories, where to put them, what page to put them on" (W: 191-192), in part because a story's placement is governed by "how much attention" (W: 193) the staff wants to bring to it. Jimmy stated that "there's a reason [stories] go on the front page" (J: 221) of the newspaper: those stories are on "important subject[s]" (J: 219). Interestingly, both Wayne and Jimmy imply that the journalist or the editorial staff determines a story's relative importance and, thus, its physical location in the newspaper. Marie commented that readers also decide on a story's importance (and whether or not to read it) based on the story's placement in the newspaper (M: 188-198). Although further research would be needed to establish if the determination of the journalists or staff (of a story's importance) matched that of the readers, it does seem reasonable to suggest that both the journalists and their readers use, albeit in slightly different ways, the physical placement of a particular story to establish that story's importance. In other words, the physical organization of a newspaper helps to create kairotic moments for individual stories; the newspaper's organization, like the organization of the story itself, helps create a sense of importance, a sense of "proportion," for readers.

The importance of a story within a newspaper is also established visually through the inclusion of accompanying pictures (including, but not limited to photographs, charts, and maps) and by manipulating the size and fonts of headlines. Jimmy noted, for instance, that when a "picture appears with a story . . . more people read the story" (J: 232-233). Similarly, the relative size of the headlines associated with particular stories helps the audience differentiate which stories are more important than others. Thus, "due measure" (i.e., "proportion") is gauged by readers based on the visual impact of the headlines. A similar judgment is made by readers when a picture is placed with the text. Wayne commented that, in keeping with his statement cited in the preceding paragraph, that the newspaper staff frequently debates on "what size headlines" and whether or not a picture should be used (W: 192). Like the organization of the story itself and the newspaper as a whole, it seems likely that readers use various visual elements (e.g., pictures and headlines) to establish a sense of "proportion" or relative importance among the stories included within the newspaper. If in fact, readers use either story or newspaper organization and/or visual elements to judge the importance of stories, then it also seems reasonable to suggest that the *kairos* construct can be used as a tool for evaluation. Such an evaluation however differs in significant, if fairly subtle, ways from the use of *kairos* (as a tool for evaluation) conducted by various contemporary scholars (e.g., Doheny-Farina, 1992, Dunmire, 2000, C. Miller, 1992). The evaluation done by readers is conducted, relatively speaking, much nearer to the time of production than that evaluation done by rhetorical analysts. Moreover, readers presumably engage the text for much different reasons than scholars *qua* analysts and, accordingly, readers likely employ much different criteria for their evaluation. Readers are, perhaps most importantly, better able to judge the appropriateness of a particular discourse because they are temporally situated closer to the authors; they are more likely than rhetorical scholars, in other words, to share the same social, political, and material context with the writers.[4]

Various visual elements, like those found in newspapers (e.g., pictures and headlines), help individuals decide where to direct their attention. Such voluntary attention is, according to Vygotsky (1929-d/trans. 1981, 1930a/trans. 1999), a higher order psychological process, one that develops only after individuals (and specifically children) begin to assimilate and use language (i.e., for Vygotsky, "speech" or the "word.") Vygotsky claims that as language first develops in children it has an "initial function . . . as a means of directing attention" (1929-d/trans. 1981, p. 214). Language shares this function with gesture, which can also be used to direct attention. Of course, both gesture and language, as well as other sign systems, are culturally specific (see, for example, McNeil, 1992, on gesture.) These similarities lead Vygotsky (1929-d/trans. 1981) to conclude that cultural mediation is fundamental to the development of voluntary attention, as this development requires artificial stimuli (i.e., signs) which are culturally produced and reproduced (pp. 195-199). Following Vygotsky's line of argument, the voluntary attention of the reader is mediated by the cultural artifact in question (i.e., the newspaper) and, more specifically, by the newspaper's organization, the story's organization, and the placement and size of pictures and headlines (among other visual elements). If, as I have demonstrated above, each of the items noted just previously is used by a reader to gauge a story's importance and, at least indirectly, help the reader establish a sense of "due measure" or "appropriateness" (i.e., establish a kairotic moment), and if each item is culturally specific, then it would follow that kairotic moments are also culturally specific. (This point will be discussed more thoroughly in Chapter 7.)

---

## Notes

1. In this regard, R. J. Bracewell (personal communication, August 29, 2003) noted that the "touchstone example" of a durable *kairos* is the obituary, for which background copy is prepared for publicly prominent individuals long in advance of and in preparation for their demise. Such pre-copy is designated, in Canadian journalism at least, as 'm-copy,' where the 'm' may stand for 'morgue,' which is the colloquialism for the archives of a newspaper." Relatedly, the journalist interviewed by Bracewell and Breuleux (Bracewell & Breuleux, 1994) was writing a story on a summit between the then current leaders of the United States and Russia. Interestingly, neither the summit nor the story

would "happen" until the following week. The journalist was, as becomes evident from the partial transcript provided, using his knowledge of the various actants (i.e., the two leaders, the history of past summits and meetings, current political, economic, and military trends, etc.) to determine how to frame the story. The journalist was, in other words, forecasting opportunity.

2. My argument here is that *kairos* functions as a symbolic (as opposed to a material) tool. As a symbolic tool, *kairos* bounds up individual knowledge and experience with regards to recognizing a kairotic moment and acting appropriately within it (i.e., by planning and carrying out a proportionate action.)

3. The identification of this gap in the scholarship was, in fact, a key impetus to the work that led up to and includes this project.

4. It is, unfortunately, beyond the scope of this project to ground this argument empirically. As noted previously, however, contemporary students of writing and rhetoric who have used *kairos* as a tool for evaluation have not yet provided either theoretical or empirical support for their transformative treatment of the construct.

# 7

# Concluding Time

I begin this chapter with some trepidation as I am uncertain, to paraphrase Aristotle, if enough has been said at present on the subject at hand. Nevertheless, I am encouraged somewhat by my own understanding of the moment for, at this moment, there seem to be a number of forces coming to bear on my own discursive production, forces which seem to necessitate or at least precipitate an end or a conclusion. Not surprisingly, this closing chapter presents a number of final comments on various topics raised previously in this volume and attempts to bring a certain level of closure or completeness to those topics. Further, this chapter discusses both various possibilities for further research in this and related areas and various limitations of this project.

## Findings Time

This project was undertaken, at least in part, in an attempt to better define or explain the *kairos* construct. As I discussed previously, contemporary scholars of writing and rhetoric have employed *kairos* for a number of purposes. However, they have generally failed to attend to the differences in the construct as it is treated across various (and largely classical Greek) rhetorical systems. These scholars have, for instance, glossed the significant differences in the definition of *kairos* as advanced by, chiefly among others, Plato and Gorgias. Thus, instead of attending to such differences, modern students of writing and rhetoric typically have put forth a rather homogenous definition of the construct, a homogenous definition that does not capture the nuances of the writing practices of the journalists reported on in this volume. Indeed it is unlikely such a singular definition ever could, based as it is in the works of the classical Greek scholars for whom *kairos* was a tool for the production of oral discourse.

The astute reader will no doubt have noticed certain similarities and convergences between Plato's conception of *kairos* and my "external model" as well as between Gorgias' conception and my "internal model." My constructs are unique, however, in at least three important ways. First, they are based in, or derived from, empirical data. Second, they specifically connect *kairos* with the production of printlinguistic texts, a connection that had only been assumed previously. Finally, the three "models" I have proposed more adequately represent how practicing writers understand and use *kairos*. Certainly, by advancing a rather singular characterization of the *kairos* construct, modern rhetorical scholars have failed to fully explicate the important ways in which the principles of "right timing" and "proportion" operate in at least one "real world" workplace.

The workplace in question, of course, is the newsroom of a major daily paper. It is not, however, entirely the province of journalism majors. Two of the three journalists interviewed graduated with other degrees (one in English and one a dual major in English and communications), albeit degrees that are in many respects fairly similar to a journalism degree. Yet, despite the differences in their educational backgrounds, each of the journalists apparently employed at various times three distinct conceptions of *kairos* during the production of text. Based on the evidence at hand, however, it is impossible to surmise when, in developmental terms, each of the journalists acquired their understandings of *kairos*. I have of course argued previously that an individual's understanding and application of the rhetorical construct *kairos* likely follows developmentally that individual's understanding and application of the human performance construct "kairos." Unfortunately, however, it is beyond the scope of this project to pinpoint when, in ontogenesis, an understanding of the rhetorical construct *kairos* develops and how such an understanding is used during the myriad of situations which might (at least potentially) benefit from the production of discourse.

A number of scholars (see, e.g., Doheny-Farina, 1992; Dunmire, 2000; and C. Miller, 1992) have argued that the rhetorical construct *kairos* impacts the discursive practices of individuals in areas as diverse as non-profit organizations, health care, and molecular biology. Although I have criticized some of these studies for failing to provide supporting empirical data, they still, nonetheless, suggest that *kairos* might figure more prominently in writing than had been understood previously. The results of this study suggest that the *kairos* construct is significant in journalism, adding another "workplace" to the ones listed immediately above. If the construct does figure importantly in the writing undertaken across such a variety of workplaces then it might be important enough, as Kinneavy (1986) has already suggested, to teach a *kairos*-based composition sequence at the college level. On the one hand, Kinneavy's position is bolstered somewhat by the data collected for this project, namely, that only one of the three journalists had a degree in journalism. Yet, all three employed *kairos* during the production of text. If *kairos* is a vital component of the writing practices in journalism as well as in other workplaces that new college graduates are likely to find themselves, then it may be important enough to teach. However, on the other hand, as I mentioned in the preceding paragraph, this project does not address when individuals develop their understandings of the rhetorical construct *kairos*. Unfortunately, none of the studies mentioned above take up such a question either. Thus, although the data gathered here supports Kinneavy's (1986) assertion that *kairos* is important enough to teach, there is currently no data available (if only because no studies, to my knowledge, have specifically focused on this question) which suggest that the construct should be taught at the college level and not at either the elementary or secondary level. (Curiously, if unfortunately, Kinneavy provides only anecdotal evidence to support his claim.)

As I noted in Chapter Two, Kinneavy (1986) bases his *kairos*-based composition program on the productive aspects of the construct, aspects often overlooked by other contemporary students of rhetoric and writing. In Chapter Two I also argued that *kairos*, as initially conceived by the classical Greek thinkers, was a tool for the production of oral discourse. Further, I demonstrated that those modern scholars who were using the *kairos* construct as a tool for the post hoc evaluation of written discourse had failed to provide either the theoretical or empirical data necessary to support their appropriation of the construct. As my analyses of the data show, the journalists apparently did not use their understandings of *kairos* as tools for evaluation; rather, they used such understandings as tools for production. Although the journalists seemed to "evaluate" their texts based on their understandings of "right timing" and "proportion," such evaluations were always done before or during text production. In other words, *kairos* was always tied to the generation of discourse. At no time did the journalists report that they used their understandings of *kairos* to evaluate the appropriateness of a written text after that text had been produced (which for the journalists was synonymous with publication.) Nonetheless, the data suggest that *kairos* can be linked to written texts; however, the data also suggest that *kairos* can only be linked to the production of written texts, and not to their post hoc evaluation.

Although his focus on the productive aspects of *kairos* is rather unique within contemporary rhetorical scholarship, Kinneavy (1986) also collapses, as do numerous other modern scholars, many of the differences encountered in the various definitions of the construct as they are advanced by the classical Greek scholars. In fact, as I noted previously, many contemporary students of writing and rhetoric rely on a rather uniform definition of *kairos*, a definition that fails to capture how the construct is operationalized by practicing writers. The three journalists I interviewed do not rely on a single definition of *kairos*. Instead, they apparently employ three distinct conceptions of the construct as part of their writing practices. Two of these, namely, the "standard" external model and the internal model, accord well generally with the ideas advanced by Plato and Gorgias, respectively, concerning the construct. The third, namely, the "durable" external model, does not, as best as I can discern, appear elsewhere in the literature on *kairos*, be that literature classical or modern in origin.

The texts of Gorgias, the relativist, and those of Plato, the idealist, are often set against each other by modern scholars, their various conceptions read as oppositional. Such is certainly true in regards to their respective conceptions of *kairos*: Gorgias maintains that *kairos* is dependent on the actions of the rhetor while Plato maintains that *kairos* is independent of the rhetor. In some ways then, the significance of this third model of *kairos* is vested, to paraphrase Charles Sanders Peirce very poorly, in its "thirdness." That is, its significance is due in part to the fact that it is the third of three conceptions, all of which are relied upon at various times by the journalists to determine the "right timing" or "due measure" of a particular story. At least in the newsroom there is not an "either-or" position on the "true" definition of *kairos*. Rather there is a "both-and" position at work. This latter position allows for both the "standard" external and internal models *as well as* the "durable" external model first discussed in Chapter Six.

In her article on the role of *kairos* in science, C. Miller (1992) recasts the "debate" between Bitzer (1968) and Vatz (1973) on rhetorical exigence in terms of *kairos*.[1] In their original terms, Bitzer held that rhetorical exigence was an objective or external feature (in relationship to the rhetor) while Vatz maintained it was a subjective or internal feature of the situation. Thus, Bitzer is often credited with an idealistic/Platonic perspective while Vatz is associated with a relativistic/Gorgian perspective. Consigny (1974) offered a conciliatory solution to the debate, suggesting that rhetorical exigence was created, in part, by external features as well as the actions of the rhetor. His resolution generally accords well with the findings I have presented here, in so far as *kairos* (or rhetorical exigence in the original terminology) can apparently be created by both the writer as well as actants external to the writer. Nonetheless, Consigny's proposal seems based on an "always-both" position (i.e., *kairos* is always created by both objective and subjective factors) that appears to conflict with the conceptions of *kairos* actually held and used by the journalists studied. C. Miller (1992) has suggested, drawing from both Consigny's (1974) work and her own study, that *kairos* "holds in productive suspension, the apparently objective and subjective dimensions of context, emphasized, respectively, by Bitzer and Vatz" (C. Miller, 1992, pp. 323-324).

As I have pointed out previously, however, the writers I studied rely on a three-part conception of *kairos* wherein the individual "parts" may or may not work together simultaneously towards the construction of a kairotic moment. In other words, the journalists seemingly invoke the different aspects of their three-part conception as needed based on the particular writing task at hand. Accordingly, it seems reasonable to suggest that *kairos* not only "holds in . . . suspension, the . . . objective and subjective dimensions of context" (C. Miller, 1992, pp. 323-324) but that it also "holds in suspension" a "durable" dimension, a dimension more permanent in nature than the objective dimension mentioned by C. Miller. Thus, it may be that C. Miller understated the situation somewhat when she wrote that "*kairos* teaches us some things about the complex nature of rhetorical context" (p. 323; emphasis in the original.) My findings suggest, in fact, that the nature of a (or *the*) rhetorical context may be more complex than previously theorized.

Of note here too is the tool-like function of *kairos*, a function only hinted at thus far in this chapter. The construct itself does not of course "hold in suspension" the three dimensions of context noted above. Rather, at least in this case, it is the journalists who use their understandings of *kairos* to "suspend" the dimensions of context. In other words, the journalists seemingly use their understandings of "right timing" and "proportion" to help them negotiate between their context and their production of text. Understanding and using *kairos* as a symbolic tool suggests that the rhetorical construct *kairos* likely develops during human ontogenesis from similar principles that operate in other performance domains. That is, it seems likely, as I demonstrated in Chapter Four, that humans use their understandings of "right timing" and "proportion" to help them solve problems and complete tasks across a number of domains. Ultimately, then, both the rhetorical construct *kairos* and the general performance construct "kairos" are used by individuals to mediate between context and production.

## Furthering Time

As a rhetorical construct, *kairos* allows rhetors to situate themselves and their production of text within a larger context. Carter (1988) suggests that *kairos*, as envisioned by Gorgias, allowed rhetors in a "relativistic world [to] ethically choose among competing *logoi*" (p. 103). A similar point is made by Sipiora (2002b) who argues that within Plato's conception of rhetoric, *kairos* can be defined as the "measurement of the discourse [against] the souls of the auditors" (p. 117). In other words, *kairos* connects the rhetor to the particularities of the situation at hand. The "ability" of *kairos* to help forge such a connection is not surprising if, as I have argued above, an individual's understanding and employment of the rhetorical construct *kairos* derives from similar principles governing general human performance. On such a view, these principles, namely, those of right timing and due measure, would also help individuals situate their behavior within larger contexts. They would, as C. Miller (1992) claims, "[hold] in productive suspension, the apparently objective and subjective dimensions of context" (pp. 323-324). Here, however, Miller is chiefly concerned with those aspects of context that are social in nature. Thus, *kairos* becomes synonymous with the term *rhetorical exigence*."[2]

*Kairos*, as presently conceived, may be in fact synonymous with *rhetorical exigence*. However, such a conception is unduly narrow for at least two significant reasons mentioned above. First, the etymological studies of Onians (1951) and Liddell and Scott (1846) suggest that the word *kairos* is intimately associated with at least two domains of human performance, neither of which are, significantly, dependent on rhetorical or discursive practices for their successful completion. Second, as I argued previously, it seems likely that the rhetorical construct *kairos* develops from a similar construct that governs general human performance. Unfortunately, I believe that our current narrow conception curtails the possibilities that a more broadly conceptualized *kairos* may have on our understandings of a number of areas important to scholars of rhetoric and writing.

One impact of an expanded notion of *kairos* would be in writing pedagogy[3] Earlier, drawing on cognitive psychology for the second explanation on the development of right timing and proportion, I explicitly linked the general human performance construct "kairos" with the cognitive psychology construct *expertise*. Moreover, as the two constructs began to converge, I implied that an understanding of the two principles of "kairos" was essential to the development of expertise. In other words, I suggested that an "expert," regardless of domain, must develop his knowledge of timing and proportion in order to plan and act properly "in the moment" of a given situation. If we accept that one of our goals as instructors is to develop a certain level of expertise within our students, then it follows that we must attend to and foster our students' understandings of right timing and proportion. Such is apparently the case regardless of the specific area of expertise we seek to develop, be that area composition, chemistry, or cross-country running. Understanding the principles of right timing and proportion, be they part of the "kairos" construct or the *kairos* construct, is intimately linked to the development of domain-specific expertise. Kinneavy (1986), who first identified the link between the rhetorical construct *kairos* and the college composition classroom, argues that *kairos* is conceptually dense enough and holds out enough promise that it should underlie the pedagogy of all writing instruction. Kinneavy's call has not been, to the best of my knowledge, implemented on any significant scale. This may well be as it should for there is little empirical evidence that suggests, in developmental terms, that the college classroom is the proper or ideal place to first teach *kairos*. Kinneavy, unfortunately, provides only anecdotal evidence for his claim. The arguments I presented above, on the development of "kairos" and its transition into *kairos*, are theoretical in nature and do not explore when such a transition takes place during ontogeny. Thus, while I support in general terms Kinneavy's call for the incorporation of *kairos* into our writing classrooms (and beyond), I believe that further research in these areas is necessary before more definitive conclusions can be reached.

The study of *context* is a second area of scholarly interest likely to be affected by a more expansive *kairos* construct. One prevailing trend in such work has been to focus on context as a social phenomenon, with the subsequent examination of how context then influences textual production (see, for example, Brandt, 1986; Faigley, 1985, and Odell, 1985.) Some more recent studies have, however, attempted to revitalize the importance of context's more material aspects in relationship to writing and other acts of meaning-making (see, for example, Chin, 1994; Haas, 1996; and Medway, 1996) without downplaying the role of context's more social aspects. Both the social and material aspects of context would seem to have some bearing on an individual's understanding of *kairos*, and her subsequent employment of *kairos* as a symbolic tool which assists in the generation of discourse. In other words, for example, an understanding of the "social" context of a given organization may help an individual determine if now is the "right time" to put forth a new proposal that is likely to generate controversy. Likewise, an understanding of the "material" context of a particular workplace may help an individual determine the best way to bring attention to (i.e., "proportion") a specific part of a report (e.g., by using an alternative organizational pattern or a brighter color paper.) Ultimately, it seems reasonable that a broader conception of *kairos*, a conception which incorporates both the "kairos" construct of general performance (a perspective grounded in material human performance) with that of the rhetorical *kairos* (a perspective grounded in rhetorical or discursive (i.e., social) performance), would allow for more integrated studies of both the material and social aspects of context and their relationships to writing.

A broader conceptualization of *kairos* is also likely to affect at least one other area of scholarship or, perhaps more concisely, an area of scholarly debate worthy of discussion, namely, the debate centered on "social" versus "cognitive" models of writing process. As with the study of context, an expanded notion of *kairos* would seem to hold some promise for reconciling, at least partially, the two models. Although any number of reasons led initially to the rather binary opposition between the social and the cognitive models of writing, the polarity is firmly entrenched in the works of a number of contemporary scholars (see, for example, Bizzell, 1982; Faigley, 1985, 1986; Nystrand, 1986). Bizzell (1982) suggests, for example, that social models of writing are "outer-directed" while cognitive models are "inner-directed." More specifically, social models focus on "thinking and language use" as they are bound to "a social context that conditions them" (p. 217) while cognitive models focus on internal, "universal, fundamental structures" (p. 217) that individuals rely on during the completion of particular writing tasks. Interestingly, Bizzell turns to Vygotsky for support of her theory that social models of writing are superior to cognitive ones. According to Bizzell, Vygotsky's ideas on thought and language "suggest . . . not only that we should not separate planning and translating [from the writing process] but also that we should understand them as conditioned by social context" (p. 224). "Planning" and "translating" are, of course, components of the cognitive model of writing; they cannot be, on Bizzell's view, purely "localized" inside the mind of an individual.

As I noted earlier, children apparently acquire an understanding of "kairos"—the principles of timing and proportion in human performance—and apply their understandings in order to plan and to solve problems before they acquire language. Only later during ontogeny does this aspect of "practical intellect" (Vygotsky, 1930a/trans. 1999, p. 13) transform and develop into an understanding of timing and proportion during rhetorical or discursive performance (i.e., into an understanding of the rhetorical construct *kairos*.) This transformation occurs as the line of the development of practical intelligence merges with the line of the development of language; it is the transformation of practical intellect by verbal speech (and other sign systems) which, according to Vygotsky, leads to the development of higher order psychological functions in children. On this matter Bizzell (1982) notes that "as Vygotsky emphasizes, with the advent of verbal thought the very nature of language-using processes changes. The writing process can only take place after this change occurred" (p. 224). However, Bizzell's contention overstates Vygotsky's position, especially as Vygotsky apparently did not study the effects of writing on higher psychological functions; his primary emphasis was always on the relationship of verbal speech (i.e., the "word") and the development of cognitive functions. This focus undoubtedly influenced, at least in part, those scholars who have chosen to label Vygotsky a "cognitive psychologist" (see, among others, Joravsky, 1989; Yaroshevsky, 1989).

Regardless of his label, Vygotsky as well as others working within the cultural-historical tradition of psychology suggest that the principles of timing and proportion first develop in individuals in non-rhetorical areas of human performance and are only later applied to rhetorical performances. Perhaps most importantly, since such principles develop before the acquisition of speech or the acquisition of writing, at least two features of discursive performance (the penultimate "social" act as described by Bizzell and others) are learned prior to the acquisition of language. These features—timing and proportion—are first learned through practical activity (i.e., problem-solving) which requires children to plan and then to translate their plans into action. Such practical activity is not oriented socially in as much as it is geared towards the completion of a personal goal that is formulated without language (and indeed before language acquisition.) Certainly, children interact with their material environment, including any other individuals which may be present. However these interactions are non-social, especially in Vygotsky's view, as the children are not yet engaged in symbolic activity which is, for Vygotsky, generally initiated by facile language users (e.g., parents and older siblings). In other words, and somewhat more concisely, the cognitive "skill" of problem-solving develops before the social "skill" of language. Further, at least one aspect of this cognitive "skill" (i.e., an understanding of timing and proportion, especially as such understanding impacts an individual's ability to plan, to translate the plan into action, and to act) is then transformed and developed as one aspect of the later social "skill."

*Kairos*, then, in its best known incarnation as the rhetorical construct embodying the principles of timing and proportion, provides a link between what Bizzell (1982) describes as "inner-directed" (i.e., cognitive) and "outer-directed" (i.e., social) theories of writing processes. Exploiting and expanding this link could ultimately lead to the development of a more robust model of writing processes, a model both more likely to reflect how individuals write and more likely to prove helpful to our students. Further theoretical and applied study is, of course, necessary but both seem potentially very beneficial. "Kairos" and *kairos*, when integrated productively, offer us, as teachers of writing, the ability to better assist our student writers say what is going on inside their heads at the proper time and in the proper manner given the larger social contexts in which their discursive performance is situated. They already have this skill and have applied it countless times in various situations; we have only to guide students as they learn to apply this skill in those situations which call for rhetoric and writing.

A number of additional questions have also arisen over the course of this project, questions which address topics and issues perhaps more interdisciplinary in nature than those discussed above. Future explorations and investigations of these topics and issues would seem, however, to have some promise for furthering our understandings of the field of writing and rhetoric.

(1)   At what point in ontogeny does the rhetorical construct *kairos* develop?

(2) Do similar conceptions of *kairos* (as identified here) operate in other workplaces?
(3) Can we better define what specific actants help to create kairotic moments, how they do so (i.e., through collision or collusion or both), what relationships obtain between various actants and human actors, etc.?
(4) Assuming that *kairos* should be taught explicitly in schools, when should it be taught? (The answer to this question depends, in part, on the answers to the first three questions.)
(5) Can we better specify the roles of "right timing" and "proportion" in the development of expertise (as an important construct in cognitive science)?[4]
(6) How culturally specific is the rhetorical construct *kairos*?
(7) Finally, what can other domains of knowledge add to our discussions of *kairos*?[5]

## Limiting Time

The findings reported in this volume are limited, unfortunately, in several significant ways. Some of these limiting factors are connected to, or arise from, my reliance solely on journalists to generate data. In other words, this study may be restricted in terms of its generalizability or applicability to other types of workplaces. The viability of this project may also be restricted because of my exclusive use of experienced journalists. Obviously, the inclusion of journalists with a greater variety of skill and experience levels might significantly change my data and findings. Still, however, the focus on the journalists provided me with the data needed to connect empirically understandings of *kairos* with the production of written text, a connection that had not been adequately supported either empirically or theoretically in previous scholarship (see my critiques of this scholarship in Chapter One and especially Chapter Two.) Much of this previous scholarship also used *kairos* as a tool for the post hoc evaluation of written text. Here, too, my focus on journalists and their writing practices did not provide the data necessary to support the use of *kairos* in an evaluation capacity. Seemingly such data would only come from studying various "consumers" of printlinguistic texts. In this specific case, further research into the writing and evaluation activities of newspaper editors as well as the evaluation activities of newspaper readers might provide the data necessary to link the *kairos* construct and evaluation. Finally, this project is also limited in that it does not empirically link the development of the human performance construct "kairos" with the development of the rhetorical construct *kairos* (although it does so in a preliminary fashion theoretically.) The longitudinal study seemingly necessary to make such a link was well beyond the scope of this project.

## Some Final Thoughts

Although the connection of what I have called the human performance construct "kairos" with the rhetorical construct *kairos* was only made at a theoretical level, I believe, nonetheless, that the argument is reasonably sound and cohesive. Certainly, as I noted just above, the connection might possibly be supported through empirical data. Still, notwithstanding the results of such a study, this project suggests that discursive performance likely follows from, or at least in this case follows the same principles as, general human performance in the material world. This claim, of course, reconciles fairly easily with any number of research traditions in psychology and cognitive science. It does not, on the other hand, dovetail well with the working assumptions often proffered by those who loosely label themselves as "social constructionists" and especially with those that Bruffee (1986) suggests "[understand] reality, knowledge, thought, facts, texts, selves, and so on as community-generated and community-maintained linguistic entities" (p. 774). The "hard-line" extension of such claims is that the material world, indeed reality itself, is composed of nothing but language; in other words, the word comes before action. This project, in one small way, suggests that the opposite perspective more accurately represents the way that the relationships which obtain between humans, the material world, and language develop over time.

These relationships, or at least our understandings of them, would seem to have some impact on our current pedagogical practices as well as our current theories of learning and writing (and perhaps the concomitant activity of reading). For instance, these findings suggest that more attention should be paid to the embodied nature of meaning making (specifically writing) and the ways in which human development changes, alters, or reinforces particular modes or methods of meaning making. Relatedly, this project also points to the inadequacy of those current approaches to writing which are based on either a "cognitive" or a "social" model. The rhetorical construct *kairos* functions as something of a mediational tool for the journalists I studied, allowing them to situate themselves (or, more specifically, their texts) within the larger material world. The various perspectives of "right timing" and "proportion" that the journalists routinely employed gave them both ways to understand the impact of various material and social actants on their production of text and ways to understand how their (individual) production of text affected the culture around them. In other words, *kairos* seems to "operate" at the intersection or junction of the individual (i.e., the "cognitive") and the cultural (i.e., the "social"). If for no other reason than this ability, as C. Miller (1992) put it, to "[hold] in . . . suspension the . . . objective and subjective dimensions of context" (pp. 323-324), *kairos* seems a construct important enough to teach in our schools. It is, at any rate, certainly worthy of further study.

## Notes

1. See, also, Dunmire (2000) for similar treatments of the Bitzer and Vatz pieces.

2. See Bitzer (1968) and Vatz (1973; rptd. 1995) for the original "debate" on rhetorical exigence. The first conflation of *kairos* with rhetorical exigence can be found in Kinneavy (1986) and subsequently in C. Miller (1992) and Doheny-Farina (1992).

3. I am using "writing pedagogy" rather broadly here to indicate the teaching of writing at any level and within/through any department; I am not using the phrase as a synonym for the teaching of first year composition courses.

4. The astute reader will no doubt have noticed that my elaboration of the *kairos* construct began to converge in important ways with constructs from different disciplines and research traditions, perhaps mostly notably with the construct of expertise and Bourdieu's (1990) construct of *habitus*.

5. Specifically here I am interested in how Festinger's (1957, 1964) theories on conflict dissonance as well as various works in linguistic anthropology (see, for example, Philips, 1974; Rosaldo, 1989) might help us profitably expand and apply our current conceptions of *kairos*.

# References

Akhundov, M. (1986). *Conceptions of time and space: Sources, evolution, directions* (C. Rougle, Trans.). Cambridge, MA: MIT Press.
Aristotle. (trans. 1994). *Art of rhetoric* (J. Freese, Trans.). Cambridge, MA: Harvard University Press.
Aristotle. (trans. 1941). Topica (W. Pickard-Cambridge, Trans.). In R. McKeon (Ed.), *The basic works of Aristotle* (pp. 187-206). New York: Random House.
Atkinson, J. & Heritage, J. (1984). Transcript notation. In J. Atkinson & J. Heritage (Eds.), *Structures of social action: Studies in conversation analysis* (pp. ix-xvi). Cambridge: Cambridge University Press.
Bannerth, E. (1973). *Islamische Wallfahrtsstatten Kairos*. Wiesbaden: Harrassowitz.
Barr, J. (1969). *Biblical words for time*. London: S. C. M. Press.
Bateson, G. (1972). *Steps to an ecology of mind*. New York: Ballantine Books.
Baumlin, J. (2002). Ciceronian decorum and the temporalities of Renaissance rhetoric. In P. Sipiora & J. Baumlin (Eds.), *Rhetoric and kairos* (pp. 138-164). Albany, NY: State University of New York Press.
Bitzer, L. (1968). The rhetorical situation. *Philosophy and rhetoric*, *1*, 1-14.
Boeckl, M. (1993). *Kairos: Die Sammlung Otto Mauer im Wiener Dommuseum: Erzbischöfliches Dom und Diözesanmuseum, Wien, Museum Moderner Kunst—Stiftung Wörlen, Passau*. Vienna: VBK Wien.
Bourdieu, P. (1990). *The logic of practice* (R. Nice, Trans.). Stanford, CA: Stanford University Press.
Bracewell, R. & Breuleux, A. (1994). Substance and romance in analyzing think-aloud protocols. In P. Smagorinsky (Ed.), *Speaking about writing: Reflections on research methodology* (pp. 55-88). Thousand Oaks, CA: Sage.
Bruffee, K. (1986). Social construction, language, and the authority of knowledge: A bibliographical essay. *College English*, *48* (8), 773-790.
Carlson, R. (1997). *Experienced cognition*. Mahwah, NJ: Lawrence Erlbaum Associates.
Carter, M. (1988). *Stasis* and *kairos*: Principles of social construction in classical rhetoric. *Rhetoric Review*, *7*, 97-112.
Cazden, C. B. (1996). Selective traditions: Readings of Vygotsky in writing pedagogy. In D. Hicks (Ed.), *Discourse, learning, and schooling* (pp. 165-185). Cambridge: Cambridge University Press.
Chase, W. & Simon, H. (1973). Perception in chess. *Cognitive Psychology*, *4*, 55-81.

Clifford, J. (1986). Partial truths. In J. Clifford & G. Marcus (Eds.), *Writing culture: The poetics and politics of ethnography* (pp. 1-26). Berkeley: University of California Press.

Consigny, S. (1974). Rhetoric and its situations. *Philosophy and Rhetoric*, 7, 175-186.

Consigny, S. (2001). *Gorgias: Sophist and artist*. Columbia, SC: University of South Carolina Press.

Cook, A. (1925). Appendix A: Kairos. In *Zeus: A study in ancient religion* (Vol. 1, pt 2) (pp. 859-868). Cambridge: Cambridge University Press.

Croissant, J., & Restivo, S. (1995). Science, social problems, and progressive thought: Essays on the tyranny of science. In S. Star (Ed.), *Ecologies of knowledge: Work and politics in science and technology* (pp. 39-87). Albany, NY: State University of New York Press.

Cullman, O. (1950). *Christ and time: The primitive Christian conception of time and history* (F. Filson, trans.). Philadelphia: Westminister.

Danièlou, J. (1953). Le *kairos* de la messe d'après les Homélies sur l'incompréhensible de St. Jean Chrysostome. In F. Arnold & B. Fischer (Eds.), *Die Messe in der Glaubensverkündigung: Kerygmatische Fragen* (pp. 71-78). Freiburg: Herder.

Das, J., Kar, B., & Parrila, K. (1996). *Cognitive planning: The psychological basis of intelligent behavior*. Thousand Oaks, CA: Sage Publications.

Davies, K. (1990). *Women, time and the weaving of the strands of everyday life*. Aldershot, UK: Avebury.

deGroot, A. (1966). Perception and memory versus thought: Some old ideas and recent findings. In B. Kleinmuntz (Ed.), *Problem solving* (pp. 19-50). New York: Wiley.

De Vogel, C. (1966). *Pythagoras and early Pythagoreanism* (I. De Vries-Kerruish & B. Hijmans, Trans.). Netherlands: Van Gorcum.

Diels, H. & Kranz, W. (1951-1954). *Die Fragmente der Vorsokratiker* (7th ed.). Berlin: Weidmann.

Doheny-Farina, S. (1992). The individual, the organization, and *kairos*: Making transitions from college to careers. In S. Witte, N. Nakadate, & R. Cherry (Eds.), *A rhetoric of doing: Essays on written discourse in honor of James L. Kinneavy* (pp. 293-309). Carbondale, IL: Southern Illinois University Press.

Dunmire, P. (2000). Genre as temporally situated social action: A study of temporality and genre activity. *Written Communication*, 17 (1), 93-138.

Ehrenwald, J. (1969). Hippocrates' '*kairos*' and the existential shift. *The American Journal of Psychoanalysis*, 29, 89-93.

Erikson, E. (1963). *Childhood and society* (2nd ed.). New York: Norton.

Festinger, L. (1957). *A theory of cognitive dissonance*. Stanford, CA: Stanford University Press.

Festinger, L. (1964). *Conflict, decision, and dissonance*. Stanford, CA: Stanford

University Press.
Freeman, K. (1949). *The pre-Socratic philosophers* (2nd ed.). Oxford: Basil Blackwell.
Freeman, K. (1962). *Ancilla to the pre-Socratic philosophers: A complete translation of the fragments in Diels, Fragmente der Vorsodratiker* (K. Freeman, trans.). Oxford: Basil Blackwell.
Gardner, R. (2001). *When listeners talk: Response tokens and listener stance.* Philadelphia: John Benjamins Publishing Company.
Gates, R. (1990). Understanding writing as an art: Classical rhetoric and the corporate context. *Technical Writing Teacher, 28*, 50-60
Gauvain, M. (1999). Everyday opportunities for the development of planning skills: Sociocultural and family influences. In A. Goncu (Ed.), *Children's engagement in the world: Sociocultural perspectives* (pp. 173-201). Cambridge: Cambridge University Press.
Gentner, D. (1988). Expertise in typewriting. In M. Chi, R. Glaser, & M. Farr (Eds.), *The nature of expertise* (pp. 1-21). Hillsdale, NJ: Lawrence Erlbaum Associates.
Glaser, B. & Strauss, A. (1967). *The discovery of grounded theory: Strategies for qualitative research.* New York: Aldine De Gruyter.
Glick, J. (1997). Prologue. In *The collected works of L. S. Vygotsky, Vol 4: The history of the development of higher mental functions* (R. W. Rieber, Ed.), (pp. v-xvi). New York: Plenum.
Golden, J., Berquist, G., & Coleman, W. (1976). *The rhetoric of Western thought.* Dubuque, IA: Kendall/Hunt.
Goldwert, M. (1991). Kairos and Eriksonian psychology. *Perceptual and Motor Skills, 72*, 553-554.
Goody, J. (1986). *The logic of writing and the organization of society.* Cambridge: Cambridge University Press.
Goody, J. (1977). *The domestication of the savage mind.* Cambridge: Cambridge University Press.
Gorgias. (trans. 1949a). Encomium of Helen. In J. Hawthorne (Trans.), *Gorgias of Leontini: A critical appraisal with translation and commentary of the extant fragments* (pp. 76-81). Unpublished dissertation, University of Chicago.
Gorgias. (trans. 1949b). Funeral oration. In J. Hawthorne (Trans.), *Gorgias of Leontini: A critical appraisal with translation and commentary of the extant fragments* (pp. 52-53). Unpublished dissertation, University of Chicago.
Gorgias. (trans. 1949c). The defense of Palamedes. In J. Hawthorne (Trans.), *Gorgias of Leontini: A critical appraisal with translation and commentary of the extant fragments* (pp. 97-106). Unpublished dissertation, University of Chicago.

Gorgias (trans. 1962). Funeral oration. In K. Freeman (Trans.), *Ancilla to the pre-Socratic philosophers: A complete translation of the fragments in Diels, Fragmente der Vorsodratiker* (pp. 129-130). Oxford: Basil Blackwell.

Haas, C. & Witte, S. (2001). Writing as embodied practice: The case of engineering standards. *Journal of Technical and Business Communication, 15* (4), 413-457.

Hainline, R. (1980). *Kairos*: A Jungian view of time. *The American Journal of Psychoanalysis, 40*, 325-333.

Havelock, E. (1986). *The muse learns to write: Reflections on orality and literacy from antiquity to the present.* New Haven, CT: Yale University Press.

Hawthorne, J. (1949). *Gorgias of Leontini: A critical appraisal with translation and commentary of the extant fragments.* Unpublished dissertation, University of Chicago.

Hayes, J. (1981). *The complete problem solver.* Philadelphia: The Franklin Institute Press.

Helsley, S. (1996). *Kairos.* In T. Enos (Ed.), *Encyclopedia of rhetoric and composition: Communication from ancient times to the information age* (pp. 371-372). New York: Garland.

Hughes, J. (2002). *Kairos* and *decorum*: Crassus Orator's speech in *de lege Servilia*. In P. Sipiora & J. Baumlin (Eds.), *Rhetoric and kairos* (pp. 128-137). Albany, NY: State University of New York Press.

Isocrates. (trans. 1956a). *Antidosis* (G. Norlin, Trans.). Cambridge, MA: Harvard University Press.

Isocrates. (trans. 1956b). *Against the Sophists* (G. Norlin, Trans.). Cambridge, MA: Harvard University Press.

Isocrates. (trans. 1961). *Panegyricus* (G. Norlin, Trans.). Cambridge, MA: Harvard University Press.

Jaques, E. (1982). *The form of time.* New York: Crane Russak.

Joravsky, D. (1989). *Russian psychology: A critical history.* Oxford: Basil Blackwell.

Kaufer, D. & Carley, K. (1993). *Communication at a distance: The influence of print on Sociocultural organization and change.* Hillsdale, NJ: Lawrence Erlbaum.

Kelman, H. (1960). '*Kairos*' and the therapeutic process. *Journal of Existential Psychiatry, 1*, 233-269.

Kelman, H. (1969). *Kairos*: The auspicious moment. *The American Journal of Psychoanalysis, 29* (1), 59-83.

Kennedy, G. (1972). Gorgias (G. Kennedy, trans.). In R. Sprague (Ed.), *The older sophists* (pp. 30-67). Columbia, SC: University of South Carolina Press.

Kennedy, G. (1980). *Classical rhetoric and its Christian and secular tradition from ancient to modern times*. Chapel Hill, NC: University of North Carolina Press.

Kerferd, G. (1981). *The sophistic movement*. Cambridge, UK: Cambridge University Press.

Kinneavy, J. (1979). The relation of the whole to the part in interpretation theory in the composing process. In D. McQuade (Ed.), *Linguistics, stylistics, and the teaching of composition* (pp. 292-312). Akron, OH: L&S.

Kinneavy, J. (1986). *Kairos*: A neglected concept in classical rhetoric. In J. Moss (Ed.), *Rhetoric and praxis: The contribution of classical rhetoric to practical reasoning* (pp. 79-105). Washington, DC: Catholic University of America Press.

Kinneavy, J. (1987). *Greek rhetorical origins of Christian faith: An inquiry*. New York: Oxford University Press.

Kinneavy, J. & Eskin, C. (1994). *Kairos* in Aristotle's *Rhetoric*. *Written Communication*, *11* (1), 131-142.

Lakoff, G. & Johnson, M. (1980). *Metaphors we live by*. Chicago: University of Chicago Press.

Lakoff, G. & Johnson, M. (1999). *Philosophy in the flesh: The embodied mind and its challenge to Western thought*. New York. Basic Books.

Lannon, J. (1997). *Technical writing* (7th ed.). New York: Longman.

Latour, B. (1987). *Science in action: How to follow scientists and engineers through society*. Cambridge, MA: Harvard University Press.

Leontyev, A. N. (1959a/trans. 1981). *Problems of the development of the mind* (M. Kopylova, Trans.). Moscow: Progress. (Russian original published in 1959 as *Problemy razvitiya psikhiki*)

Levi, D. (1924). Il concetto di kairos e la filosofia di Platona. *Rendiconti della Reale Academia Nazionale dei Lincei classe di scienzia morali* RV 33, 93-118.

Levina, R. E. (1968/trans. 1981). L. S. Vygotsky's ideas about the planning function of speech in children (J. V. Wertsch, Trans.). In J. V. Wertsch (Ed. & Trans.), *The concept of activity in Soviet psychology* (pp. 281-299). Armonk, NY: M. E. Sharpe. (Russian original published in *Voprosy psikhologii*, No. 4, pp. 105-115)

Liddell, H. & Scott, R. (1846). *Greek English Lexicon*. New York: Harper & Brothers.

Luria, A. R. (trans. 1981). *Language and cognition* (J. V. Wertsch, Ed.; no translator given). New York: Wiley-Interscience.

Markel, M. (2001). *Technical communication*. Boston: Bedford/St. Martin's.

McNeill, D. (1992). *Hand and mind: What gestures reveal about thought*. Chicago: University of Chicago Press.

Miller, B. (1987). Heidegger and the Gorgian kairos. In C. Kneupper (Ed.), *Visions of rhetoric: History, theory, and criticism* (pp. 169-184). Arlington, TX: Rhetoric Society of America.

Miller, C. (1992). *Kairos* in the rhetoric of science. In S. Witte, N. Nakadate, & R. Cherry (Eds.), *A rhetoric of doing: Essays on written discourse in honor of James L. Kinneavy* (pp. 310-327). Carbondale, IL: Southern Illinois University Press.

Myers, G. (1996). Out of the laboratory and down to the bay: Writing in science and technology studies. *Written Communication, 13* (1), 5-43.

O'Meara, D. (1989). *Pythagoras revisited: Mathematics and philosophy in late antiquity*. Oxford: Clarendon Press.

Ong, W. (1982). *Orality and literacy: The technologizing of the word*. New York: Routledge

Onians, R. (1951). *The origins of European thought about the body, the mind, the soul, the world, time, and fate*. New York: Arno.

Ortony, A. (1993). Metaphor, language, and thought. In A. Ortony (Ed.), *Metaphor and thought* (2nd ed.) (pp. 1-16). Cambridge: Cambridge University Press.

Philips, S. (1974). Warm Springs 'Indian time': How the regulation of participation affects the progression of events. In R. Bauman & J. Sherzer (Eds.), *Explorations in the ethnography of speaking* (pp. 92-109). Cambridge: Cambridge University Press.

Pickering, A. (Ed.). (1992). *Science as practice and culture*. Chicago: University of Chicago Press.

Plato. (trans. 1981). *Five dialogues: Euthyphro, Apology, Crito, Meno, Phaedo* (G. Grube, Trans.). Indianapolis, IN: Hackett Publishing.

Plato. (trans. 1995). *Phaedrus* (H. Fowler, Trans.). Cambridge, MA: Harvard University Press.

Plato. (trans. 1958). *Phaedrus* (W. Helmbold and W. Rabinowitz, Trans.). Indianapolis: Bobbs-Merrill.

Plato. (trans. 1997). Timaeus (D. Zeyl, Trans.). In J. Cooper (Ed.), *Plato: Complete works* (pp. 1224-1291). Indianapolis, IN: Hackett Publishing.

Pohlenz, M. (1933). *To Prepon*: Ein Beitrag zur Geschichte des griechischen Geisters. In *Nachrichten von der Gesellschaft der Wissenschaften zu Goettingen, Philologisch-historische Klasse, Heft I* (pp. 53-92).

Posner, M. (1988). Introduction: What is it to be an expert? In M. Chi, R. Glaser, & M. Farr (Eds.), *The nature of expertise* (pp. xxix-xxxvi). Hillsdale, NJ: Lawrence Erlbaum Associates.

Potter, J. & Wetherell, M. (1987). *Discourse and social psychology: Beyond attitudes and behavior*. London: Sage.

Prince, H. (1978). Time and historical geography. In T. Carlstein, D. Parkes, & N. Thrift (Eds.), *Making sense of time* (pp. 17-37). New York: John Wiley & Sons.

Rämö, H. (1999). An Aristotelian human time-space manifold: From chronochora to kairotopos. *Time & Society, 8* (2), 309-328.

Rämö, H. (2001). Ancient ideas in a new setting: *Chronos, kairos, chora,* and *topos* in a postindustrialized world. In M. Soulsby and J. Fraser (Eds.), *Time: Perspectives at the millennium (The study of time x)* (pp. 237-246). Westport, CT: Bergin & Garvey.

Rosaldo, R. (1989). *Culture and truth: The remaking of social analysis.* Boston: Beacon Press.

Rostagni, A. (1922). Un nuovo capitolo nella storia della retorica e della sofistica. *Studi italiani di filologica classica,* n.s. 2, 148-201.

Ryle, G. (1949). *The concept of mind.* Chicago: University of Chicago Press.

Scholnick, E. & Cookson, K. (1994). A developmental analysis of cognitive semantics: What is the role of metaphor in the construction of knowledge and reasoning? In W. Overton & D. Palermo (Eds.), *The nature and ontogenesis of meaning* (pp. 109-128). Hillsdale, NJ: Lawrence Erlbaum.

Salthouse, T. (1984). Effects of age and skill in typing. *Journal of Experimental Psychology, General, 113,* 345-371.

Schegloff, E. (2001). Accounts of conduct in interaction: Interruption, overlap and turn-taking. In J. Turner (Ed.), *Handbook of sociological theory* (pp. 287-321). New York: Kluwer Academic.

Schegloff, E. (1984). On some questions and ambiguities in conversation. In J. Atkinson & J. Heritage (Eds.), *Structures of social action: Studies in conversation analysis* (pp. 28-52). Cambridge: Cambridge University Press.

Scribner, S. (1983; rpt. 1997). Mind in action: A functional approach to thinking. In E. Tobach, R. Falmagne, M. Parlee, M. Martin, & A. Kapelman (Eds.), *Mind and social practice: Selected writings of Sylvia Scribner* (pp. 296-307). Cambridge: Cambridge University Press.

Scribner, S. (1985; rpt. 1997). Thinking in action: Some characteristics of practical thought. In E. Tobach, R. Falmagne, M. Parlee, M. Martin, & A. Kapelman (Eds.), *Mind and social practice: Selected writings of Sylvia Scribner* (pp. 319-337). Cambridge: Cambridge University Press.

Searle, J. (1993). Metaphor. In A. Ortony (Ed.), *Metaphor and thought* (2nd ed.) (pp. 83-111). Cambridge: Cambridge University Press.

Sheard, C. (1993). Kairos and Kenneth Burke's psychology of political and social communication. *College English, 55* (3), 291-310.

Simon, H. (1989). *Models of thought* (Vol. 2). New Haven, CT: Yale University Press.

Sipiora, P. (2002a). Introduction: The ancient concept of *kairos.* In P. Sipiora & J. Baumlin (Eds.), *Rhetoric and kairos* (pp. 1-22). Albany, NY: State University of New York Press.

Sipiora, P. (2002b). *Kairos*: The rhetoric of time and timing in the New Testament. In P. Sipiora & J. Baumlin (Eds.), *Rhetoric and kairos* (pp. 114-127). Albany, NY: State University of New York Press.

Smith, B. (1921). Gorgias: A study of oratical style. *Quarterly Journal of Speech Education, 7,* 335-359.
Smith, J. (1986). Time and qualitative time. *Review of Metaphysics, 40,* 3-16.
Smith, J. (1969). Time, times, and the 'right time': Chronos and kairos. *The Monist, 53,* 1-13.
Spradley, J. (1972). Foundations of cultural knowledge. In J. Spradley (Ed.), *Culture and cognition: Rules, maps, and plans* (pp. 3-38). Prospect Heights, IL: Waveland Press.
Star, S. (1995). The politics of formal representations: Wizards, gurus, and organizational complexity. In S. Star (Ed.), *Ecologies of knowledge: Work and politics in science and technology* (pp. 88-118). Albany, NY: State University of New York Press.
Star, S. (1991). Power, technology, and the phenomenology of conventions: On being allergic to onions. In J. Law (Ed.), *A sociology of monsters: Essays on power, technology, and domination* (pp. 26-56). London: Routledge.
Strauss, A. (1987). *Qualitative analysis for social scientists.* Cambridge: Cambridge University Press.
Strauss, A. & Corbin, J. (1994). Grounded theory methodology: An overview. In N. Denzin & Y. Lincoln (Eds.), *Handbook of qualitative research* (pp. 273-285). Thousand Oaks, CA: Sage.
Sullivan, D. (1992). *Kairos* and the rhetoric of belief. *Quarterly Journal of Speech, 78* (3), pp. 317-332.
Svennevig, J. (1999). *Getting acquainted in conversation: A study of initial interactions.* Philadelphia: John Benjamins Publishing Company.
Swales, J. (1984). Research into the structure of introductions to journal articles and its application to the teaching of academic writing. In R. Williams, J. Swales, & J. Kirkman (Eds.), *Common ground: Shared interests in ESP and communication studies* (pp. 77-86). New York: Pergamon
Swales, J. (1981). *Aspects of article introductions.* Birmingham, UK: Language Studies Unit, University of Aston, Birmingham.
Swales, J. & Najjar, H. (1987). The writing of research article introductions. *Written Communication, 4,* 175-191.
Thompson, R. (2002). Ralph Waldo Emerson and the American *kairos.* In P. Sipiora & J. Baumlin (Eds.), *Rhetoric and kairos* (pp. 187-198). Albany, NY: State University of New York Press.
Tillich, P. (1967). *Systematic theology: Three volumes in one.* Chicago, IL: University of Chicago Press.
Tuffin, K. & Howard, C. (2001). Demystifying discourse analysis: Theory, method and practice. In A. McHoul & M. Rapley (Eds.), *How to analyse talk in institutional settings* (pp. 196-205). London: Continuum.
Untersteiner, M. (1954). *The sophists* (K. Freeman, Trans.). New York: Philosophical Library.

Valsiner, J. (1988). *Developmental psychology in the Soviet Union.* Bloomington, IN: Indiana University Press.
Vatz, R. (1973; rpt. 1995). The myth of the rhetorical situation. In W. Covino & D. Jolliffe (Eds.), *Rhetoric: Concepts, definitions, boundaries* (pp. 461-467). Boston: Allyn & Bacon.
Vygotsky, L. S. (1926/trans. 1993). Defectology and the study of the development and education of abnormal children (J. E. Knox & C. B. Stevens; Trans.). In *The collected works of L. S. Vygotsky, Vol 2: The fundamentals of defectology* (R. W. Rieber & A. S. Carton, Eds.) (pp. 164-170). New York: Plenum. (Russian original, probably *Defektologija i uchenie o razvitie i vospitani nenormal'nogo rebenka*, was likely written around 1926)
Vygotsky, L. S. (1929/trans. 1981). The development of higher forms of attention in childhood. In J. V. Wertsch (Ed. & Trans.), *The concept of activity in Soviet psychology* (pp. 191-240). Armonk, NY: M. E. Sharpe. (Russian original was apparently written in 1929 and first published in 1960 in *Razvitie vysshikh psikhicheskikh* [The Development of Higher Mental Functions])
Vygotsky, L. S. (1930a/trans. 1999). Tool and sign in the development of the child (M. J. Hall, Trans.). In *The collected works of L. S. Vygotsky, Vol 6: Scientific legacy* (R. W. Rieber, Ed.) (pp. 1-68). New York: Plenum. (Russian original, *Orudie i znak* [Tool and sign], is a 1930 ms published for the first time in the Russian edition of *The Collected Works*, Vol. 6 [i.e., *Sobranie sochinenij, 1984b, Tom 6*])
Vygotsky, L. S. (1930b/trans. 1997a). Preface to Köhler (R. van der Veer, Trans.). In *The collected works of L. S. Vygotsky, Vol 3: Problems of the theory and history of psychology* (R. W. Rieber & J. Wollock, Eds.) (pp. 175-194). New York: Plenum. (Russian original is a *"predislovie"* to the 1930 Russian translation, *Issledovanie intellekta chelovekopodobnykh obez'jan*, of W. Köhler's *Intelligenzprüfungen an Menschenaffen* [Study of the Intellect of Human-Like Simians])
Vygotsky, L. S. (1934a/trans. 1986). *Thought and language.* (A. Kozulin, Trans.) Cambridge, MA: The MIT Press. (Russian original published in 1934 as *Myschlenie i rech'*)
Vygotsky, L. S. (1934b/trans. 1998). The problem of age (M. J. Hall, Trans.). In *The collected works of L. S. Vygotsky, Vol 5: Child psychology* (R. W. Rieber, Ed.) (pp. 187-205). New York: Plenum. (Russian original, titled *Problema vozrasta*, is an ms from the Vygotsky family archives)
Wardy, R. (1996). *The birth of rhetoric: Gorgias, Plato and their successors.* New York: Routledge.
Wertsch, J. (1991). *Voices of the mind: A sociocultural approach to mediated action.* Cambridge, MA: Harvard University Press.

White, E. (1994) Kairos. In S. Macey (Ed.), *Encyclopedia of time* (pp. 332-333). New York: Garland.
White, E. (1987). *Kaironomia: On the will-to-invent*. Ithaca, NY: Cornell University Press.
Whitrow, G. (1976). 'Becoming' and the nature of time. In M. Capek (Ed.), *The concepts of space and time: Their structure and their development* (pp. 525-532). Boston: D. Reidel.
Wilson, F. (1998). *The hand*. New York: Vintage Books.
Witte, S., Stephenson, H., & Bracewell, R. (In progress). *Cultural-historical psychology, cognitive science, and the study of writing*.
Yaroshevsky, M. G. (1989). *Lev Vygotsky* (S. Syrovatkin, Trans.). Moscow: Progress. (Russian original apparently published during the same year as the translation)

# Name Index

Akhundov, M., 10-12
Aristotle, 8-9, 22, 23, 24, 77-78, 83
Atkinson, J., 58
Avery, O., 28, 29-30
Bannerth, E., 12n1
Barr, J., 1
Bateson, G., 53
Baumlin, J., 8, 14n11
Berquist, G., 12n1
Bitzer, L., 30, 86, 93n1, 93n2
Bizzell, P., 50, 89-90
Boeckl, M., 12n1
Bourdieu, P., 93n4
Bracewell, R., 54n6, 80n1
Brandt, D., 88
Breuleux, A., 80n1
Bruffee, K., 92
Carley, K., 26
Carlson, R., 52, 53
Carter, M., 1, 2, 5, 6, 13n7, 17, 18, 31n2, 87
Cazden, C., 25, 50
Chase, W., 42
Chin, E., 88
Cicero, 9
Clifford, J., 33
Coleman, W., 12n1
Consigny, S., 6, 13n9, 86
Cookson, K., 1
Cook, A., 1
Corbin, J., 58, 60
Crick, F., 28, 29
Croissant, J., 71
Cullman, O., 12n1, 36-38
Daniélou, J., 12n1, 36-37
Das, J., 42
Davies, K., 34
DeGroot, A., 52
DeVogel, C., 17-18
Diels, H., 13n9
Doheny-Farina, S., 2, 6, 27-28, 29, 30, 80, 84, 93n2

Dionysius, 6, 31n4
Dunmire, P., 1, 2, 34, 80, 84, 93n1
Ehrenwald, J., 12n1
Erikson, E., 39-40
Eskin, C., 2, 8
Faigley, L., 50, 88-89
Festinger, L., 93n5
Freeman, K., 6, 13n9, 31n2
Gardner, R., 58
Gates, R., 27
Gauvain, M., 46-47
Gentner, D., 52, 53
Glaser, B., 58, 60
Glick, J., 12
Golden, J., 12n1
Goldwert, M., 39
Goody, J., 26
Gorgias, 6-9, 18-20, 22, 23, 24, 30, 31n4, 78, 83, 85, 87
Gurevich, Y., 11-12
Haas, C., 53, 88
Hainline, R., 12n1, 39-40
Havelock, E., 26
Hawthorne, J., 13n9
Hayes, R., 51
Helmbold, W., 31n5
Helsley, S., 13n7
Heritage, J., 58
Hesiod, 4, 5
Howard, C., 59
Hughes, J., 9
Homer, 4
Iamblichus, 17
Isocrates, 8, 23-24, 77
Jacques, E., 1
Johnson, M., 9-12
Joravsky, D., 50, 89
Kar, B., 52
Kaufer, D., 26
Kelman, H., 12n13, 39-40
Kennedy, G., 12n1, 13n9

# Name Index

Kerferd, G., 6
Kielholz, A., 39
Kinneavy, J., 1, 2, 6-9, 12n2, 13n7, 18, 20-21, 24, 25-27, 30, 31n5, 31n7, 31n9, 31n10, 33-36, 42, 84-85, 88, 93n2
Kranz, W., 13n9
Lakoff, G., 9-12
Lannon, J., 26
Latour, B., 70
Leont'ev, A. N., 16, 49-50, 54n3, 54n4
Levi, D., 7
Levina, R., 46
Liddell, H., 13n6, 16, 45, 73, 87
Luria, A., 46-47, 50, 54n3
Markal, M., 26
Marx, K., 54n4
McNeil, D., 53, 80
Medway, P., 88
Miller, B., 1, 2, 30
Miller, C., 1, 2, 28-30, 31n11, 33, 80, 84, 86-87, 92, 93n2
Myers, G., 70-71
Najjar, H., 25
Nystrand, M., 50, 89
Odell, 88
O'Meara, D., 31n2
Ong, W., 26
Onians, R., 4, 6, 13n6, 13n8, 15-16, 33, 45, 73, 87
Ortony, A., 9
Palamedes, 19-20
Parrila, K., 52
Phillips, S., 93n5
Pickering, A., 70
Pierce, C., 85
Pindar, 4, 5
Plato, 7-8, 13n10, 20-22, 23, 24, 35, 42, 43n1, 52, 70, 73, 77-78, 83, 85, 87
Pohlenz, M., 12n1
Posner, M., 52

Potter, J., 58-59
Prince, H., 34
Pythagoras, 5, 17-18
Rabinowitz, W., 31n5
Rämö, H., 1, 2
Restivo, S., 71
Rosaldo, R., 93n5
Rostagni, A., 5, 18, 31n1
Ryle, G., 53
Salthouse, T., 52
Schegloff, E., 58
Scholnick, E., 1
Scott, R., 13n6, 16, 45, 73, 87
Scribner, S., 52
Searle, J., 10-12
Sheard, C., 2
Simon, H., 51, 52
Sipiora, P., 4, 7, 20-21, 31n5, 31n6, 31n8, 87
Smith, B., 6, 13n9
Smith, J., 33-36, 37, 42
Socrates, 7, 13n10, 20
Spradley, J., 31n7
Star, S., 71
Stephenson, H., 54n6
Strauss, A., 58-60
Sullivan, D., 2
Svennevig, J., 58
Swales, J., 25
Thompson, R., 36
Tillich, P., 12n1, 36-38
Tuffin, K., 59
Turner, M., 9
Untersteiner, M., 1, 5, 9, 13n7, 17, 18-19, 21, 31n1, 31n2, 31n7
Valsiner, J., 43n3
Vatz, R., 30, 86, 93n1, 93n2
Vygotsky, L., 25, 40-42, 43, 45-46, 48-50, 54n3, 54n4, 74, 80, 89-90
Wardy, R., 12n1
Watson, J., 28, 29
Wertsch, J., 40

Wetherell, M., 58-59
White, E., 4, 20
Whitrow, G., 11-12, 14n12
Wilson, F., 53
Witte, S., 53, 54n6
Yaroshevsky, M., 50, 89

# Subject Index

actor network theory, 70-73; and classical rhetoric, 71
agency, and *kairos*, 15, 19-20, 30, 35-38, 62-63, 66-67
*akairos*, 21, 24
Christian theology, 36-38; eschatological view of history, 37; typology, 38
*chronos*, 35; relationship to *kairos*, 1, 33-34, 37
cognitive science (See psychology, cognitive.)
construct, defined 1-2, *kairos* as 1-2, 6, 29
context, 88-89 (See also *kairos*, as situational context.)
*decorum*, 8-9, 13
discourse community, 27
distributed cognition, 42
education, 40-41
embodied practice, 53, 54n7
*eukairos*, 21
expertise, 29, 52-53, 87 (See also planning competency.)
grounded-theory approach, 58-61 (See also research design, data analysis methodology.)
internalization (interiorization), 46
journalism, and *kairos*, 62-67
*kairoi*, 37-38
Kairos (mythological god), 39
*kairos* (rhetorical construct), and actor network theory, 71-73; and archery, 4, 12n5, 15-16, 33; and Aristotle, 8, 22; as capacity, 18-20; and Christian theology, 12n1, 12n2, 36-38; as construct, 1-2, 6, 29, 75; contemporary rhetorical scholarship on, 25-30, 83-85; defined, 1, 4, 12n6, 85; durable external model of, 69-70, 72-74, 85-86; early meanings, 4-5, 12n6, 15-17; and education, 26, 31n7, 31n9, 31n10, 40-42, 84-85; etymology, 4, 12n6, 15-17, 87; as evaluation tool, 15-30, 34-38, 75-77, 81n4, 85; and Gorgias, 6-7, 18-20, 83, 85, 87; and historical analysis, 12n1, 33-36; and human performance, 2, 5, 8, 12n5, 30, 33-43, 73, 87; impact on textual production, 65-67; internal model of, 62, 66, 69-75, 83, 85-86; and Isocrates, 8, 23-24; and ontogeny, 2, 12n5, 30, 31n7, 34-35, 67n5, 73-75; and organization, 64, 78-79; and Plato, 7-8, 18-20, 42; as precept, 18-20, 21; as production tool, 2, 4, 15-30, 34-36, 38, 62-66, 74, 81n2, 85-87; as proportion/due measure, 1-2, 4, 12n3, 25, 27; 63-64, 67, 77-80; and psychoanalysis, 12n1, 38-40; and Pythagoras/Pythagoreans, 17-18; relationship to *decorum* and *prepon*, 8-9; and rhetorical exigence, 86-87; and rhetorical performance, 2, 8, 12n5, 19-30, 35; 62-67, 87; as right timing/timing, 1-2, 4, 8, 10, 19-25, 27, 34, 36-37, 39; 62-63, 65-67; and Roman rhetorics, 8-9, 12n4; as situational context, 5, 6, 18, 26-27, 30, 64-65, 86, 88-89; and social origins, 16, 66 80; spatial aspects of, 4-7, 10-11, 15; standard external model of, 62, 67, 69-75, 83, 85-86; and style, 63-64, 77-78; temporal aspects of, 4-8, 10-11, 15, 33; and temporal stability, 28-29, 31n12, 62, 65-66, 69-70, 72-73,

80n1; translations of, 12n3, 13, 37; and visuals/graphics, 79-80; and weaving, 4, 12n5, 15-16, 33, 73; and writing, 2, 12n4, 22-30, 61-67, 69-70, 71-73, 75-77; and writing pedagogy, 87-88, 90; and writing process, 89-90; and the zone of proximal development, 40-42

"kairos" (human performance construct), 48-50, 53-54, 75, 82, 88, 90; as construct, 45, 54n1

*logoi/logos*, 6, 21, 87

metaphor, and *kairos*, 9-12, 15; spatial, 10-12; temporal, 10-12

metonymy, 10-11

opportunity, 13n8

planning/plans, 50-53; and evaluation, 50-52; and *kairos*, 18, 42, 87-88; and "kairos," 47-48, 51-52

planning competency, 52 (See also expertise)

practical intelligence (practical intellect), 48-49

*prepon (to prepon)*, 8-9

problem-solving, and *kairos*, 28, 42, 90; and "kairos," 49, 90

psychology, Vygotskian (cultural-historical), 45-50, 89-90; cognitive, 50-54

research design, data analysis methodology, 58-61; data sources, 56-57, 67n4; data transcription, 57-58, 67n3, 67n4; description of participants, 55-56; initial questions, 3; later questions, 90-91; limitations of, 91

speech, and development of higher psychological functions, 45-46, 49; and planning, 46-47

time, 1, 10-11, 13n12

tool, and *kairos* 15-30; material aspects of, 16; social aspects of, 16

*topoi/topos*, 7

writing process, 89-90

zone of proximal development, 40-42; definition of, 40; and "kairos," 48

## About the Author

Hunter Stephenson comes to the field of rhetoric and composition rather circuitously. After receiving a B.S. in Marine Engineering from the United States Coast Guard Academy, he was an active duty Coast Guard officer for nine years, most of which was spent conducting drug and migrant interdiction operations in the Caribbean Sea.

Stephenson returned to academia after leaving the Coast Guard, completing his M.A. (in English) and Ph.D. (in Rhetoric and Composition) at Kent State University. His research interests include workplace literacy and writing, classical rhetoric, distributed cognition, and cultural-historical psychology. He is currently an assistant professor of writing at the University of Houston Clear Lake. This is his first book.

www.ingramcontent.com/pod-product-compliance
Lightning Source LLC
Chambersburg PA
CBHW021131300426
44113CB00006B/387